Frances Eales
Steve Oakes

speakout

Elementary
Workbook

PEARSON
Longman

CONTENTS

1 WELCOME   PAGE 5

1.1 GRAMMAR | present simple: *be*
VOCABULARY | greetings; countries and nationalities
READING | wonky-pedia
WRITING | capital letters

1.2 GRAMMAR | *this/that*, *these/those*; possessives
VOCABULARY | objects
LISTENING | interviews at an airport

1.3 FUNCTION | making requests
VOCABULARY | tourist places; at a hotel
LEARN TO | listen for key words

2 LIFESTYLE   PAGE 10

2.1 GRAMMAR | present simple: *I/you/we/they*
VOCABULARY | activities
LISTENING | doing a course

2.2 GRAMMAR | present simple: *he/she/it*
VOCABULARY | daily routines; jobs
READING | a hot dog seller
WRITING | *and*, *but* and *or*

2.3 FUNCTION | asking for information
VOCABULARY | the time; life at home
LEARN TO | show you don't understand

3 PEOPLE   PAGE 15

3.1 GRAMMAR | frequency adverbs; modifiers
VOCABULARY | personality
READING | HELP! forum

3.2 GRAMMAR | *have/has got*
VOCABULARY | family
LISTENING | families
WRITING | apostrophe *'s*

3.3 FUNCTION | making arrangements
VOCABULARY | time expressions; activities on
             special occasions
LEARN TO | show interest

4 PLACES   PAGE 23

4.1 GRAMMAR | *there is/are*
VOCABULARY | rooms/furniture; prepositions (1)
READING | Top tips for small rooms
WRITING | punctuation

4.2 GRAMMAR | *can* for possibility
VOCABULARY | places in a town; prepositions (2)
LISTENING | Pueblo Inglés

4.3 FUNCTION | shopping
VOCABULARY | things to buy
LEARN TO | say *no* politely in a shop

5 FOOD   PAGE 28

5.1 GRAMMAR | countable and uncountable nouns;
                 nouns with *a/an*, *some*, *any*
VOCABULARY | food/drink
READING | too busy to eat?

5.2 GRAMMAR | *how much/many*; quantifiers
VOCABULARY | containers; large numbers
LISTENING | the junk food lover's diet
WRITING | paragraphs

5.3 FUNCTION | ordering in a restaurant
VOCABULARY | restaurant words; cooking
LEARN TO | understand fast speech

6 THE PAST   PAGE 33

6.1 GRAMMAR | *was/were*
VOCABULARY | dates and times
READING | celebrities who are friends

6.2 GRAMMAR | past simple
LISTENING | adopted twins
WRITING | *because*, *so*, *and*, *but*

6.3 FUNCTION | making conversation
VOCABULARY | weekend activities
LEARN TO | keep a conversation going

Review and Check 1   PAGE 20

Review and Check 2   PAGE 38

CONTENTS

7 HOLIDAYS — PAGE 41

7.1 GRAMMAR | comparatives
VOCABULARY | travel
READING | travel partners

7.2 GRAMMAR | superlatives
VOCABULARY | places (1)
LISTENING | an audio diary
WRITING | checking and correcting

7.3 FUNCTION | giving directions
VOCABULARY | places (2)
LEARN TO | check and correct directions

10 THE FUTURE — PAGE 59

10.1 GRAMMAR | *be going to*; *would like to*
VOCABULARY | plans
READING | a lottery winner

10.2 GRAMMAR | *will*, *might*, *won't*
VOCABULARY | phrases with *get*
LISTENING | survival
WRITING | *too*, *also*, *as well*

10.3 FUNCTION | making suggestions
VOCABULARY | adjectives (2); weather
LEARN TO | respond to suggestions

8 NOW — PAGE 46

8.1 GRAMMAR | present continuous
VOCABULARY | verbs with prepositions
LISTENING | phone conversations
WRITING | pronouns

8.2 GRAMMAR | present simple/continuous
VOCABULARY | appearance; clothes
READING | the T-shirt

8.3 FUNCTION | recommending
VOCABULARY | types of film
LEARN TO | link words

11 HEALTH — PAGE 64

11.1 GRAMMAR | *should/shouldn't*
VOCABULARY | the body
READING | walking – the perfect sport?

11.2 GRAMMAR | adverbs of manner
VOCABULARY | common verbs
LISTENING | what's your real age?
WRITING | adverbs in stories

11.3 FUNCTION | offering to help
VOCABULARY | problems
LEARN TO | thank someone

9 TRANSPORT — PAGE 51

9.1 GRAMMAR | articles
VOCABULARY | transport collocations
READING | commuting

9.2 GRAMMAR | *can/can't*, *have to/don't have to*
VOCABULARY | adjectives (1)
LISTENING | the balancing scooter

9.3 FUNCTION | apologising
VOCABULARY | excuses; airport
LEARN TO | tell a long story

12 EXPERIENCES — PAGE 69

12.1 GRAMMAR | present perfect
VOCABULARY | outdoor activities
READING | a travel blog
WRITING | postcard phrases

12.2 GRAMMAR | present perfect and past simple
VOCABULARY | prepositions
LISTENING | fear or fun?

12.3 FUNCTION | telephoning
VOCABULARY | telephoning expressions; feelings
LEARN TO | say telephone numbers

Review and Check 3 — PAGE 56

Review and Check 4 — PAGE 74

1.1 WELCOME

VOCABULARY greetings

1 Put the words in the conversation in the correct order.

1 A: you? / Hi, / are / Jeff. / How
    Hi, Jeff. How are you?

2 B: thanks. / Great, / you? / are / How
    _____

3 A: is / friend, / Fine. / This / my / Marianne.
    _____

4 C: Nice / you. / meet / to
    _____

5 B: Hello, / you. / Nice / I'm / to / Jeff. / meet
    _____

GRAMMAR present simple: *be*

2 Complete the conversations with the correct form of *be*.

Ben: Hello. How are you?

Ed: Er ... hello.

Ben: Sorry, ¹ *are* you Mr and Mrs Rutter?

Ed: No, we ²_____. They ³_____ Mr and Mrs Rutter.

Ben: Oh, sorry.

Ben: Excuse me. ⁴_____ you Jerry Rutter?

Jerry: Yes.

Ben: I ⁵_____ Ben Pastor.

Jerry: Oh, hello. Nice to meet you, Ben. This ⁶_____ my wife, Sally.

Sally: Hi.

Ben: Sorry. ⁷_____ your name Sandy?

Sally: No, it ⁸_____. It's Sally.

Ben: Nice to meet you, Sally.

3 Write the conversations.

1 you / American?   *Are you American?*
   No, / I / Canadian.   *No, I'm not. I'm Canadian.*

2 he / a student?   _____
   No, / He / a teacher. _____

3 we / late?   _____
   No, / You / early.   _____

4 they / from India?   _____
   No, / They / China.   _____

VOCABULARY countries and nationalities

4A Find twelve countries in the puzzle.

G	R	E	E	C	E	C	Q	S
P	O	R	T	U	G	A	L	C
R	G	E	R	M	A	N	Y	O
U	S	O	Y	E	Q	A	J	T
S	P	C	U	X	F	D	A	L
S	A	H	V	I	Z	A	P	A
I	I	I	U	C	M	U	A	N
A	N	N	P	O	L	A	N	D
T	H	A	I	L	A	N	D	P

B Write the nationalities for the countries in the puzzle.

   Greek   _____
   _____   _____
   _____   _____
   _____   _____
   _____   _____
   _____   _____

C Complete the table with the nationalities.

1 -an / -ian	2 -ish
German	Polish
3 -ese	**4 other**
Portuguese	Greek

D ▶1.1 Listen and underline the stressed syllable in each nationality. Then listen again and repeat.

READING

5A Read the website extract and underline five mistakes.

WONKY-PEDIA

1 Michael Phelps, 8-gold-medal swimmer at the Beijing Olympic games in 2008, am from the USA.

2 Toyota and Honda are Japanese cars. Fiat and Ferrari are Italians cars.

3 Egypt, Botswana and Kenya are countries in Africa.

4 Sydney is a big city in the south-east of Australia and it's famous for the Opera House and the Harbour Bridge.

5 In New York, the taxi are yellow.

6 The Amazon and the Orinoco are rivers in South America.

7 Starbucks is American company with over 15,000 coffee houses in more than 40 countries.

8 David Beckham is a famous footballer from the Britain.

B Correct the mistakes.

*Michael Phelps **is** from the USA.*

_____

_____

_____

_____

_____

_____

WRITING capital letters

6 Complete the words with the letters in brackets. **Use capitals where necessary.**

1 _T_ his is a __hoto of __e at the __olosseum in __ome, __taly.

(t p m c r i)

2 __his is me and my __ustralian __riend, __aul. __e're in __enice.

(t a f p w v)

3 __his is __enji at a __ar in __adrid. __enji is a __tudent from __apan.

(t k b m k s j)

4 __ere is __aul again. __e's at __axim's in __aris. __axim's is a __rench __estaurant.

(h p h m p m f r)

VOCABULARY objects

1A Look at the pictures and complete the crossword.

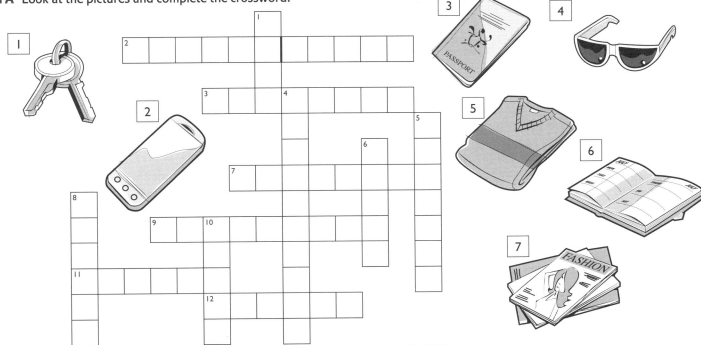

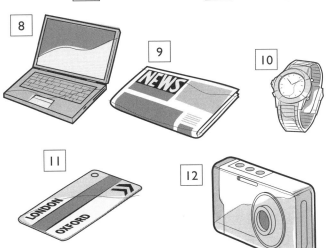

B ▶ 1.2 Listen and write the words from Exercise 1A in the correct place in the table according to the stress.

1 O	2 Oo
keys	passport

3 Ooo	4 ooO
sunglasses	mobile phone

C Listen again and repeat.

LISTENING

2A ▶ 1.3 Listen to interviews with three passengers at an airport and complete the table.

	Passenger 1	Passenger 2	Passenger 3
Nationality	Canadian		
Tourist (T) or on business (B)?		T	

B Listen again. Tick the objects in the passengers' bags.

	Passenger 1	Passenger 2	Passenger 3
laptop			
newspaper			
hairbrush			
MP3 player			
sunglasses			
passport	✓		
camera			
ticket			
newspaper			
magazine			
mobile phone			
keys			

GRAMMAR *this/that, these/those*

3 Complete the sentences with *this, that, these* or *those*.

John: ¹ *These* are great sunglasses. How much are they?

Shop assistant: ²_____? They're two hundred euros.

John: Two hundred euros!

Shop assistant: But ³_____ sunglasses are only twenty euros.

John: OK. And how much is ⁴_____ magazine?

Shop assistant: ⁵_____'s two euros.

John: Two? OK, here you are.

Shop assistant: Thanks.

4A Write the sentences in the plural.

1 That CD's great!
   Those CDs are great!

2 This red pen is Anne's.
   _____

3 This isn't my key.
   _____

4 Where's that ticket?
   _____

B Write the sentences in the singular.

1 These books are very good.
   This book's very good.

2 Those aren't my files.
   _____

3 Who are those men over there?
   _____

4 Are these your photos?
   _____

GRAMMAR possessives

5 Add one apostrophe (') to each conversation.

1 A: Is this your mobile phone?
    B: No, it isn't. I think it's Jane's.

2 A: Are these DVDs yours?
    B: No, they're Suzannas.

3 A: Is your friends name Greg?
    B: Yes, Greg Hutchens.

4 A: Are these Nathans sunglasses?
    B: I don't know. Ask him.

5 A: Are your teachers photos in the book?
    B: Yes, they're on pages 17 and 18.

6 A: Where are Irenas tickets?
    B: They're on the table.

6A Change the sentences so they don't repeat the nouns.

1 These glasses are ~~my glasses~~.
   These glasses are mine.

2 These keys are your keys.
   _____

3 That bag is Jack's bag.
   _____

4 Those pencils are my pencils.
   _____

5 This mobile phone is Anita's mobile phone.
   _____

6 That magazine is your magazine.
   _____

B ▶ 1.4 Listen and check.

C Underline the letter 's' in the answers.

1 The*s*e gla*ss*e*s* are mine.

D What is the pronunciation of the letter 's'? Listen again and write /s/ or /z/. Then listen and repeat.

1 The*s*e gla*ss*e*s* are mine.
     /z/   /s//z/

VOCABULARY tourist places

1A Add the vowels in brackets.

1 snackbar c_l_c_ffees_ndwich (add **a** or **o**)

2 t_uristsh_pp_stc_rdb_tterys_uvenir (add **a** or **o**)

3 bur_ _ud_ch_ng_ _xch_ng_r_t_mon_y (add **a** or **e**)

4 tr_ _nst_t_ons_nglet_cketpl_form (add **a** or **i**)

B Circle the places and objects in Exercise 1A.

FUNCTION making requests

2A Complete the conversations with the words in the box.

| have | you | That's | euro | please | help | ~~Do~~ | Can |

Conversation 1

Tourist: Excuse me. ¹ _Do_____ you speak English?

Shop assistant: Yes. Can I ²_____ you?

Tourist: ³_____ I have these four postcards, please?

Shop assistant: OK. ⁴_____ two euros, please.

Conversation 2

Tourist: Can I ⁵_____ a coffee, ⁶_____?

Waiter: That's one ⁷_____ fifty.

Tourist: Thank ⁸_____.

B ▶1.5 Listen to the conversations in Exercise 2A. Then listen again and repeat.

LEARN TO listen for key words

3A ▶1.6 Listen and look at the menu. What do the people order? Write the food and drink for 1–6.

1 _a tomato salad_   a) € _2_____
2 _____   b) € _____
3 _____   c) € _____
4 _____   d) € _____
5 _____   e) € _____
6 _____   f) € _____

B Listen again and write the prices for a)–f).

VOCABULARY at a hotel

4 Look at the pictures and complete the places/services in a hotel.

1 st_airs_____

2 li_____

3 re_____

4 ke_____

5 pa_____

6 re_____

7 in_____
co_____

8 ro_____
se_____

MENU

✳✳✳

 Drinks

Coffee

Espresso coffee

Tea

Iced Tea

Mineral water

✳✳✳

 Rolls

Egg

Chicken

Cheese

✳✳✳

Salads

Green

Tomato

✳✳✳

 Ice cream

VOCABULARY activities

1 Complete the profile below with verbs from the box.

come listen play take drink do read watch
go eat

ALLTOGETHER.NET

Personal Profile:
Teresa Alvarez

About me
I ¹ _come_
from Mexico,
I'm twenty-three
years old and I'm
a student. I study
politics at UNAM
(the National
Autonomous
University of
Mexico). I'm
single.

Activities
I ²_____ a lot of sport – I ³_____
running every day and I ⁴_____ tennis
most weeks.

Interests
Photography: I love meeting people and I
⁵_____ photos of people all the time.
Food: I like going out to restaurants with
friends. We ⁶_____ Mexican food and
⁷_____ Mexican beer!

Favourite music
I ⁸_____ to different kinds of music, but
I really like World Music.

Favourite TV shows
I ⁹_____ a lot of American programmes.
I like *CSI* and *Friends*.

Favourite Movies
Anything with Johnny Depp!

Favourite Books
Love in the Time of Cholera by Gabriel
García Márquez. I ¹⁰_____ it every year!

2A ▶ 2.1 Listen and write the words from the box in the correct place in the table according to the stress.

~~key~~ ~~camera~~ ~~newspaper~~ sport photo magazine
coffee cinema exercise MP3 player DVD TV
nothing golf film

1 O	2 Oo	3 oO
key	camera	
4 Ooo	**5 ooO**	**6 ooOoo**
newspaper		

B Listen again and repeat.

GRAMMAR present simple: *I/you/we/they*

3 Write the questions and short answers.

1 **A:** you / eat / junk food, Juan? **B:** No / I
   Do you eat junk food, Juan? *No, I don't.*

2 **A:** you / do / a lot of sport, Kiko? **B:** Yes / I
   _____ _____

3 **A:** the students in your class / **B:** No / they
   live / near you?
   _____ _____

4 **A:** you and Clara / like / Italian **B:** Yes / we
   food?
   _____ _____

5 **A:** you / listen / Radio 5, Daniel? **B:** Yes / I
   _____ _____

6 **A:** Ursula and Hans / study / **B:** No / they
   English with you?
   _____ _____

7 **A:** I / have / classes on Saturday? **B:** No / you
   _____ _____

8 **A:** you and your family / eat / **B:** Yes / we
   together?
   _____ _____

9 **A:** Ali and Marco / play / tennis? **B:** Yes / they
   _____ _____

10 **A:** you and Ana / drink / coffee? **B:** No / we
   _____ _____

LISTENING

4A Look at the course list. Which course is good for you?

UNION COUNTY
ADULT EDUCATION COURSE LIST

Office yoga: 7.30–9p.m.
Salsa for beginners: 7–9p.m.
Digital photography: 9–12p.m.
Singing for fun: 6.30–8.30p.m.

B ▶ 2.2 Listen to the conversation. Number the courses on the list in the order the people talk about them.

C Listen again and complete the table.

	Which day?	Where?	What?
Office Yoga			stretching and relaxing exercises
Salsa for Beginners			
Digital Photography		high school	
Singing for Fun	Monday and		

D Tick one correct question from the conversation. Then correct the other five questions.

1 Which course you want to do?
   Which course **do** you want to do?
2 You like music?
   _____
3 Do you take photos?
   _____
4 Where you do work?
   _____
5 Sit you at your desk a lot?
   _____
6 What you do do in an Office Yoga class?
   _____

E Match answers a)–f) with questions 1–6 above.
a) I take them on holiday.   *3*
b) Yes, all day.
c) I don't know. Can you help me?
d) We learn exercises that you do at your desk.
e) At a bank.
f) Yes I do. I sing in the car.

GRAMMAR present simple: *I/you/we/they*

5 Look at the information about Francesco and his flatmates, Ben and Tom. Complete Francesco's sentences.

	Francesco	Ben and Tom
watch TV a lot	✓	✗
listen to the radio	✗	✓
eat in fast-food restaurants	✗	✗
drink a lot of cola	✓	✓
read computer magazines	✗	✓
go to the cinema	✗	✓
do sport	✓	✗
play video games	✓	✓

1 I _watch_____ TV a lot, but I _don't listen to____ the radio.
2 Ben and Tom _____ TV a lot, but they _____ the radio.
3 We _____ in fast-food restaurants.
4 We _____ a lot of cola.
5 Ben and Tom _____ computer magazines.
6 I _____ to the cinema.
7 Ben and Tom _____ sport.
8 We _____ video games.

VOCABULARY daily routines

1A Put the letters in the correct order to make phrases.

1 eahv fskarbeta   *have breakfast*

2 vhae hlucn   _____

3 og ot dbe   _____

4 teg emho   _____

5 avhe nndire   _____

6 tge pu   _____

7 astrt kowr   _____

8 evale meho   _____

9 nishfi rowk   _____

B Match times a)–i) with phrases 1–9.

a) 6a.m.   6

b) 7a.m.

c) 8.a.m.

d) 9.a.m.

e) 1p.m.

f) 5p.m.

g) 6p.m.

h) 8p.m.

i) 11p.m.

WRITING and, but and or

2 Join the sentences with one of the words in brackets.

1 On Monday, I leave for work at 9. I get home at 6. (and/or)

   On Monday, I leave for work at 9 and I get home at 6.

2 On Tuesday, I phone my mother. I chat with her for hours. (but/and)

   _____

3 On Wednesday, I get up early. I don't go to work – it's my free day. (or/but)

   _____

4 On Thursday, I work in the office. I work at home. (but/or)

   _____

5 On Friday, I go out late with my friends. I go to bed early. (and/or)

   _____

6 On Saturday, I play tennis with Pete at 9. I have lunch with him. (and/but)

   _____

7 On Sunday morning, I read a newspaper. It isn't in English! (but/or)

   _____

8 On Sunday afternoon, I listen to music. I watch TV. (but/or)

   _____

GRAMMAR present simple: he/she/it

3A Write the *he/she/it* form of verbs 1–12.

1 sleep   *sleeps*

2 play   _____

3 drink   _____

4 drive   _____

5 relax   _____

6 eat   _____

7 study   _____

8 know   _____

9 wash   _____

10 leave   _____

11 get   _____

12 practise   _____

B Write verbs 1–12 in the correct place in the table according to the ending.

1 /s/	2 /z/	3 /ɪz/
sleep<u>s</u>	play<u>s</u>	relax<u>es</u>

C ▶ 2.3 Listen and check. Then listen and repeat.

4 Complete the text with the present simple of the verbs in brackets.

Al is a hot dog seller in New York. Every day he ¹ *gets up* (get) at 5p.m. and ² _____ (make) dinner for his two boys – they get home from school at about 4.30. He ³ _____ (not drive) to work but ⁴ _____ (take) the bus into the city. He ⁵ _____ (start) work at 7p.m. At about 1a.m. he ⁶ _____ (have) two or three hot dogs for lunch. He ⁷ _____ (not stop) working all night. He ⁸ _____ (see) a lot of interesting things, but most people are very friendly. He ⁹ _____ (finish) work at 3 or 4a.m. On the bus he ¹⁰ _____ (not sleep) but ¹¹ _____ (read) the morning newspaper. He ¹² _____ (get) home at about 6a.m. He ¹³ _____ (have) breakfast with his family, and ¹⁴ _____ (go) to bed at about 8.30a.m. and that's the end of his day … or night.

READING

5A Read the article and answer the questions.

1 Does Al like his job?

2 Does he work at the weekend?

A NIGHT IN THE LIFE OF A HOT DOG SELLER

'In my job I meet a lot of interesting people. People like talking to me, they don't just want a hot dog, they want a conversation. It's great working at night. It's never hot, people are relaxed, and they're very hungry. Some nights I sell over 300 hot dogs. I have one customer, Hector, he's a taxi driver, he eats ten hot dogs every night. People ask me, "Al, do you like hot dogs?" Yes, of course I like them, I love them! Hot dogs are NOT junk food, they're good food. My boys love them too, and we have hot dogs for dinner every Saturday night. I don't work at the weekend, I'm with the boys all day and then sleep at night. They play football in the park, and I watch them, or I play with them. Or I go and get a hot dog!'

B Read the article again. Are sentences 1–8 true (T) or false (F)?

1 Al doesn't like people.   *F*

2 People don't talk to Al.

3 People aren't hungry at night.

4 Hector doesn't sell hot dogs.

5 Al doesn't like hot dogs.

6 Al and his boys have hot dogs for Saturday dinner.

7 Al sleeps at night at the weekend.

8 Al doesn't go to the park with his boys.

C Correct the false sentences.

1 Al likes people.

GRAMMAR present simple: *he/she/it*

6 Put the words in the correct order to make questions.

1 live / Eva / does / where?

   Where does Eva live?

2 Juanes / does / coffee / drink?

   _____

3 what / 'junk' / does / mean?

   _____

4 lunch / he / when / have / does?

   _____

5 like / she / does / popcorn?

   _____

6 read / does / which / Kay / newspaper?

   _____

7 does / how / work / Faisal / come / to?

   _____

8 your / come / does / where / car / from?

   _____

VOCABULARY jobs

7 Look at the pictures. Complete the jobs puzzle. Use the letters in the shaded squares to make another job.

Hidden job:

_____

VOCABULARY the time

1 Write the times in two different ways.

1 7.30   _It's half past seven._ / _It's seven thirty._
2 9.15   _____   _____
3 11.10 _____   _____
4 2.45   _____   _____
5 5.20   _____   _____
6 8.35   _____   _____
7 10.55 _____   _____
8 1.40   _____   _____

FUNCTION asking for information

2A Look at leaflets A–C. What are they about?

A

TRAIN TIMETABLE
London to Cambridge

| London Kings Cross | 1 _10.52_ | 11.15 |
| Cambridge | 11.54 | 2 _____ |

B

BANGKOK TEMPLE TOUR

Start time: ³_____
Finish time: ⁴_____
Tour start point: ⁵_____
Adult: ⁶_____ baht / 14 euros

C

NATIONAL BANK

Opening hours

Monday–Friday: ⁷_____ to 4p.m.
Saturday: 10a.m. to ⁸_____
Sunday: Closed

B Look at gaps 1–8 in the leaflets. Write the questions to find the information. Use the prompts below.

1 What time / leave?   _What time does the train leave?_
2 When / arrive?   _____
3 What time / start?   _____
4 When / finish?   _____
5 Where / start from? _____
6 How much / cost?   _____
7 What time / open?   _____
8 When / close?   _____

C ▶ 2.4 Underline the key word in each question in Exercise 2B. Then listen and repeat.

D ▶ 2.5 Listen and complete gaps 1–8 in the information in Exercise 2A.

LEARN TO show you don't understand

3A Listen to the conversations in Exercise 2D again. In which conversations do the people show they don't understand?

B Put the phrases in the correct order.

1 speak / you / could / slowly / sorry, / please? / more
_____

2 Wat Phra ... ? / the / me, / excuse
_____

3 you / that? / could / spell
_____

4 you / could / that? / repeat / sorry,
_____

VOCABULARY life at home

4A Complete verbs 1–10 in the table.

		Steve	Ellie	both
1	m_ake_ breakfast	✓		
2	m_____ the beds			✓
3	g_____ shopping		✓	
4	b_____ food		✓	
5	d_____ the washing	✓		
6	d_____ the ironing			✓
7	c_____ the rooms			✓
8	w_____ the floors		✓	
9	c_____ dinner	✓		
10	d_____ the washing-up	✓		

B Look at the table and complete the sentences.

1 Steve _makes breakfast_ , _does the washing_ , _____ and _____.
2 Ellie _____, _____ and _____.
3 They both _____, _____ and _____.

3.1 PEOPLE

VOCABULARY personality

1A Add the vowels.

1 knd   _kind_
2 ntllgnt   _____
3 fnny   _____
4 frndly   _____
5 tlktv   _____
6 nknd   _____
7 srs   _____
8 nhppy   _____
9 stpd   _____
10 qt   _____
11 nfrndly   _____
12 hppy   _____

B Write the adjectives from Exercise 1A in the correct group according to the stress.

1 O	2 Oo	3 oO
kind		

4 Ooo	5 oOo	6 oOoo

C ▶ 3.1 Listen and check. Then listen and repeat.

D Complete the conversations with adjectives from Exercise 1A.

1 A: I think Mark's very friendly.
 B: Really? He never talks to me! I think he's very _unfriendly_ .
2 A: Andrea's really talkative at breakfast time.
 B: Yeah, I don't like it. I like to be _____ in the mornings!
3 A: Lena's a serious student.
 B: Yes, usually, but she's sometimes very _____.
4 A: The teachers are kind to Greg.
 B: Yes, but some of the children are _____.
5 A: This cat's very stupid!
 B: Don't be horrible! I think she's very _____!
6 A: Ben's happy today.
 B: Yes, but his teacher's _____ – he's late for class!

GRAMMAR frequency adverbs

2 Underline the correct alternative.

1 Mixing yellow and red _always_ / often / sometimes makes orange.
2 The colour red often / sometimes / hardly ever means 'danger' or 'stop'.
3 Apples are sometimes / hardly ever / never purple.
4 In football, the ball is usually / hardly ever / never white.
5 A chef in a restaurant never / sometimes / always has a white hat.
6 Food is often / hardly ever / never blue.
7 Cola is always / sometimes / never brown.
8 People always / often / never drink their coffee white – with milk.
9 Taxis in New York are hardly ever / always / sometimes yellow.
10 Eggs are usually / never / hardly ever white or brown.

3A Read the emails. Are Sandy and Cristina good flatmates?

Hi Maria,

How are you? I'm fine but I've got a new flatmate, Cristina, and she's a real problem. She talks to me never. When she comes home in the evening I ask her usually about her day. She says 'fine' always and then she watches usually TV or she goes to her room to sometimes sleep! She wants hardly ever to chat. What can I do?

Sandy

Hi Zsuzsa,

How are you? I'm fine but my new flatmate, Sandy, is a real problem. She stops talking never. In the evening after classes I'm tired often. I want to usually relax in front of the TV for half an hour or I have sometimes a short rest. She wants always to talk about her day. I have hardly ever energy to listen.

That's my news. Email me soon!

Cristina

B Circle the frequency adverbs and draw a line to their correct position in the emails.

15

READING

4A Read the forum and tick the ideas you agree with.

HELP! forum

My friend Sam often asks me for money. I usually say no, but sometimes I give him ten or twenty euros. The problem is he never pays me back. I don't want to ask him but I feel bad about the whole thing. Help! (**Jon, Ontario**)

Beth writes: Talk to him about it. Tell him how you feel. You say he's your friend and real friends listen to each other. But remember, money and friends don't mix. Good luck!

Karl writes: I don't think he's a real friend. It's time to end the friendship – tell him to give you the money and then say goodbye!

Steve writes: Forget the money. Friends are everything. Money's not important – but don't give him more money!

I work with Joanne and I really like her, but we aren't friends. The problem is that <u>she</u> thinks we're friends. She often asks me to meet her after work and at the weekend. She phones me three or four times a week and she just wants to chat. Help! (**Patsy, Christchurch**)

Levente writes: Maybe it's a good idea to meet her just once at the weekend. You say you like her, well, give her a chance. Good luck!

Miki writes: That's a problem. Tell Joanne the truth – you're a friendly person but you aren't her friend!

Cynthia writes: That's really difficult. Change your telephone number ... or don't answer the phone. She needs to understand that you don't want to be friends.

B Underline two names from the forum for each sentence.

1 They're friends.
<u>Sam</u>   Joanne   <u>Jon</u>   Patsy
2 They aren't friends.
Sam   Joanne   Jon   Patsy
3 They say: Don't be friends with him/her.
Beth   Karl   Levente   Miki
4 They say: Tell the truth.
Beth   Steve   Miki   Cynthia
5 They say: Be friends with him/her.
Karl   Steve   Levente   Cynthia

GRAMMAR modifiers

5 Complete the conversations with *very* or *quite*.

Conversation 1
A: I get up early every day.
B: Oh. What time do you get up?
A: At 9a.m.
B: 9a.m.! That isn't _very_ early! That's late!
A: Well, my husband gets up at 4a.m.
B: Now that's _____ early. I get up at 7a.m.
A: OK, OK! That's _____ early.

Conversation 2
A: I love this laptop, but it's €1,000.
B: That's _____ expensive.
A: I know.
B: How about this one? It's _____ expensive, but it's a good make.
A: How much is it?
B: €600. Hey, look at this one. It's in the sale. It's only €250. That isn't _____ expensive.
A: You're right. That's a good price.

Conversation 3
A: I run ten kilometres every morning.
B: Really? How long does it take you?
A: It usually takes about 45 minutes.
B: That's _____ good. It usually take me about 55 minutes.
A: Oh. That isn't _____ fast.
B: But in a race it takes 38 minutes!
A: Wow, that's _____ good!

Conversation 4
A: What time does the film start?
B: At Rialto Cinema it starts at 11p.m.
A: Oh, that's _____ late!
B: But at Westwood Cinema it starts at 10p.m.
A: That's _____ late for me. I always get up early to go for a run.
B: Well the early show at Westwood starts at 7p.m.
A: That isn't _____ good. It's 7p.m. now.

Conversation 5
A: You never talk in class.
B: No, that's true.
A: In fact you never talk.
B: No.
A: You're a _____ quiet person.
B: That's right. I'm not _____ talkative.
A: But your English isn't bad.
B: No?
A: It's _____ good in fact. Not great, but not bad.
B: Thanks.

VOCABULARY family

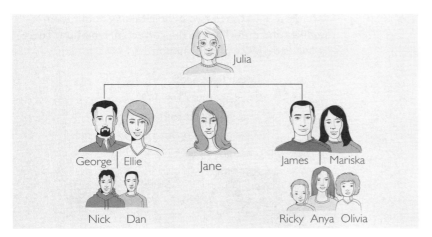

Julia

George | Ellie   Jane   James | Mariska

Nick Dan   Ricky Anya Olivia

1A Look at the family tree and complete the conversations.

Conversation 1

Jane: Chris, this is my ¹ _mother_ , Julia.

Chris: Nice to meet you, Mrs Garnet.

Jane: And this is my ² _____ George and his ³ _____, Ellie.

Chris: Hello.

Jane: And these are my ⁴ _____, Nick and Dan.

Nick: Hi.

Conversation 2

Chris: Are these your children, Mariska?

Mariska: Oh, let me introduce you. These are my ⁵ _____, Anya and Olivia, and this is my ⁶ _____, Ricky.

Ricky: Hi!

Mariska: And this is James, my ⁷ _____.

Chris: Hello, everyone.

Ricky: And that's my ⁸ _____, George and my ⁹ _____, Jane.

Chris: Yes, I know. I'm a friend of Jane's.

Ricky: And those are my ¹⁰ _____, Nick and Dan.

Conversation 3

Chris: Ellie, what's that little girl's name? I forget.

Ellie: That's my ¹¹ _____, Anya.

Chris: And her ¹² _____ are Mariska and ... ?

Ellie: James. We're a big family. A lot of names to remember!

B Look at the underlined letters. Is the pronunciation the same (S) or different (D)?

1 si**s**ter   mo**th**er   S
2 c**ou**sin   **u**ncle
3 w**i**fe   n**ie**ce
4 **au**nt   f**a**ther
5 s**o**n   h**u**sband
6 gr**a**ndfather p**a**rents
7 d**augh**ter   br**o**ther
8 n**e**phew   fr**ie**nd

C ▶ 3.2 Listen and check. Then listen and repeat.

2 Complete the sentences with family words.

1 My mother's _father_ is my grandfather.
2 My father's _____ is my sister.
3 My sister's _____ are my mother and father.
4 My children's _____ is my sister.
5 My children's _____ is my brother.
6 My mother's _____ is my cousin, Matt.
7 My father's _____ is my cousin, Nina.
8 My father's _____ is my mother.
9 My mother's _____ is my father.
10 My son's _____ are my mother and father.

GRAMMAR *have/has got*

3A Read the information in the table and complete sentences 1–8 with the correct form of *have got*.

I	a new laptop
My sister	an MP3 player
My brother	an old computer
My parents	a black car
My family	a four-room flat

1 I *'ve got*_____ a new laptop.
2 I _____ an MP3 player.
3 My sister _____ a computer.
4 My parents _____ a car.
5 My brother _____ a computer, but it's old.
6 We _____ a house.
7 We _____ a flat.
8 It _____ four rooms.

B Complete the questions and short answers. Use the information in the table.

1 *Have*_____ you *got*_____ a new laptop?
   *Yes, I have.*_____

2 _____ your brother _____ a new computer?
   _____

3 _____ you _____ a house?
   _____

4 _____ your sister _____ an MP3 player?
   _____

5 _____ your flat _____ four rooms?
   _____

6 _____ your parents _____ a black car?
   _____

4 Correct five mistakes with *have got* and *be* in each conversation.

Conversation 1
A: I haven't got a pen. ~~Are you one?~~ *Have you got one?*_____
B: No, I'm not, but I've got a pencil.
A: Has it got black?
B: No, it's got red.
A: Has it got a rubber?
B: Yes, it is.
A: Can I borrow it? Thanks.

Conversation 2
A: Have you got your camera with you?
B: No, but Fatima's an MP3 player.
A: Has it got a camera, Fatima?
C: No, it isn't. But my mobile phone's got a camera.
A: Has it got good?
C: Not really. It's very small and the pictures haven't got very good.
A: That's OK. Can you take a photo of me?
C: OK, smile! Look. You're a nice smile.

LISTENING

5A ▶ 3.3 Listen to two people talking about their families and draw lines to the correct information. There is one extra piece of information.

David   1 hasn't got a job.
         2 has got one sister.
Meg   3 has got one brother.
         4 has got five brothers.
         5 has got a good job.

B Listen again. Are the sentences true (T) or false (F)?
1 Tom is Meg's brother.   *T*
2 Meg is close to her sister.
3 Nick is David's brother.
4 Nick is quite active.
5 Jenny is David's mother.
6 David and Jenny are close.
7 Jenny's husband doesn't like his job.
8 Jenny's got three sons.

WRITING apostrophe *'s*

6A Complete the text with *'s* or *s*.

My friend ¹Jean*'s*_____ got an interesting family. Her brother ²Sam_____ super intelligent and ³he_____ got a good job with a computer company in Sydney. ⁴He_____ married and his ⁵wife_____ name is Grace. ⁶Jean_____ sister ⁷Sally_____ the funny one in the family. She ⁸love_____ telling funny stories and she ⁹work_____ as an actress with the Melbourne Theatre Company. Jean ¹⁰live_____ here in Brisbane in my friend ¹¹Keira_____ apartment.
¹²Jean_____ the 'baby' of the family. ¹³She_____ got a big heart. People always say that ¹⁴she_____ very kind.

B Match meanings a)–d) with 1–14 in Exercise 5A.
a) is   c) possessive
b) has   *1*   d) *he/she/it* form of regular verb

C Write about a friend's family. Write 60–80 words. Include information about their jobs and personalities.

VOCABULARY time expressions

1 Look at the information about Tara and complete sentences 1–8.

My week	Sun	Mon	Tue	Wed	Thu	Fri	Sat
sleep late							✓
do sport		✓		✓		✓	
have lunch at home		✓			✓		
clean the flat	the 1st and 3rd Friday of every month						
go shopping	✓	✓	✓	✓	✓	✓	✓
meet friends for dinner							✓
go to the cinema	1 or 2 times every year						
phone Mum	✓✓	✓✓	✓✓	✓✓	✓✓	✓✓	✓✓

1 Tara _sleeps_ late _once a week_ .
2 She _____ sport _____ .
3 She _____ lunch at home _____ .
4 She _____ the flat _____ .
5 She _____ shopping _____ .
6 She _____ friends for dinner _____ .
7 She _____ to the cinema _____ .
8 She _____ her mother _____ .

FUNCTION making arrangements

2 Correct the mistakes in the conversation.

A: Hi, Stefanie. Do you free tomorrow?

1 _Hi, Stefanie. **Are** you free tomorrow?_

B: Yes, I am. What you want to do?

2 _____

A: How about going a club?

3 _____

B: Mmm. That a problem. I don't like loud music.

4 _____

A: You like films?

5 _____

B: Yes, I like.

6 _____

A: How about see the new James Bond film?

7 _____

B: OK. What time do you want go?

8 _____

A: Seven good for me.

9 _____

B: OK, see us there!

10 _____

LEARN TO show interest

3 Complete the words.

1 A: We've got a new baby! A little girl!
   B: That's fa_ntastic_ ! What's her name?
2 A: I always go swimming before I go to work.
   B: That's gr_____. It's very good for you.
3 A: My sister isn't here. She isn't very well.
   B: Oh. That's a sh_____. I hope she's OK soon.
4 A: We never go on holiday. We haven't got any money.
   B: That's aw_____! Everyone needs a holiday.
5 A: Oh, no, the airport's closed and I've got a flight this afternoon.
   B: That's te_____! Why is it closed?
6 A: This is my cousin, Monika. She's a chef.
   B: That's in_____. I love cooking!
7 A: I've got a new girlfriend. She's beautiful _and_ intelligent.
   B: That's wo_____! Where's she from?

VOCABULARY special occasions

4 Look at the pictures and complete the activities.

1 d_ance_ to special m_____
2 g_____ a pr_____
3 w_____ special cl_____
4 w_____ f_____ on TV
5 h_____ a p_____
6 s_____ 'H_____ b_____'
7 in_____ gu_____
8 g_____ to a re_____
9 e_____ special f_____

VOCABULARY review

1A Add the vowels to the words in each group.

1	
tr_a_v_e_l	V
l_ ght_ r	O
w_ ll_ t	
P_ l_ nd	
s_ ndw_ ch	
w_ _t_ r	

2
n_ wsp_ p_ r
h_ _ rdr_ ss_ r
l_ st_ n t_
cr_ d_ t c_ rd
C_ n_ d_
ch_ w_ ng g_ m

3
pr_ j_ ct_ r
_ mbr_ ll_
_ cc_ _ nt_ nt
t_ k_ ph_ t_ s
h_ t ch_ c_ l_ t_
K_ r_ _ n

4
_ ng_ n_ _ r
s_ _ v_ n_ r
cl_ _ n th_ r_ _ ms
V_ _ tn_ m
m_ g_ z_ n_
ch_ ck_ n r_ ll

B In each group find: a job (J), two objects (O), a country (C) or nationality (N), a food (F) or drink (D), and a verb or verb phrase (V).

C Match stress patterns a)–d) with groups 1–4 in Exercise 1A.

a) ooO   4

b) Oo

c) oOo

d) Ooo

D ▶ RC1.1 Listen and repeat.

GRAMMAR present simple

2A Complete the text with the correct form of the verbs in brackets.

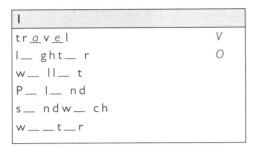

IS THIS A REAL JOB? MEET ROY, THE HOLIDAY VOLUNTEER

Roy [1]'s _____ (be) Canadian and [2]_____ (work) in a youth hostel in Corfu, Greece. He and the other hostel workers [3]_____ (be) volunteers – they [4]_____ (not get) money for their work. Every day Roy [5]_____ (get up) at six and [6]_____ (have) breakfast in the hostel. He [7]_____ (not cook) the meals. Cynthia [8]_____ (be) the chef and she [9]_____ (do) all the shopping and cooking. Every morning, Roy [10]_____ (clean) the rooms and [11]_____ (help) on the organic farm at the hostel, growing food for the guests. In the afternoons, he [12]_____ (not work) and he usually [13]_____ (go) to the beach. After dinner, he and the hostel guests often [14]_____ (chat) together. 'It [15]_____ (be) a great job,' Roy says. 'Everyone's very friendly. I [16]_____ (not want) the summer to end.'

B Write the questions.

1 How old / be / Roy?   _He's twenty-seven._

2 Where / be / he / from?   _____

3 Where / be / the hostel?   _____

4 How much / money / the volunteers / get?   _____

5 When / Roy / get up?   _____

6 Who / be / Cynthia?   _____

7 she / clean / the rooms?   _____

8 What / Roy / usually / do / in the afternoons?   _____

9 What / he and the guests / do / in the evenings?   _____

10 he / like / his job?   _____

C Answer the questions.

1 _He's twenty-seven._

2 _____

3 _____

4 _____

5 _____

6 _____

7 _____

8 _____

9 _____

10 _____

VOCABULARY personality

3A Put the letters in order to complete the riddles.

1 I never talk, but I'm not very *tqeiu* _quiet_.
2 I'm not *eellnintgit* _____, but I always know the time.
3 I'm usually quite *sisoreu* _____, but not very *nikd*
   _____ or *leirnyfd* _____.
4 I'm really *lavttikea* _____ and I never listen.
5 I'm quite *pidsut* _____, but I write in many languages.

B Match objects a)–e) with sentences 1–5 in Exercise 3A.

a) a radio   4   d) a pen
b) a watch   e) the TV news
c) a dog

GRAMMAR have/has got

4 Complete the sentences with *be* or *have/ has got*.
What's the answer to question 8?

1 My name*'s* _____ Amari.
2 I _____ one brother and one sister.
3 My mother _____ one sister.
4 She _____ (not) any brothers.
5 My mother's sister _____ Jen.
6 Jen _____ married to Henry.
7 Jen and Henry _____ two nephews and one niece.
8 _____ I a boy or a girl?

VOCABULARY / FUNCTION revision

5A Complete the poems.

Poem 1
I do*n't* _____ like my mobile ph_____.
I of_____ want to be alone.
But then my mo_____ phone, it rings.
I really, really ha_____ these th_____!

Poem 2
'I like co_____ ing and cl_____ ing, too.'
'Oh, good. The gue_____ arrive at two.
You ma_____ a cake and wa_____ the floor
and wake me up at ha_____ past fo_____!'

Poem 3
'Co_____ I have a sandwich, pl_____?'
'Of co_____, what kind? Meat or ch_____?'
'Oh, I'm not sure, so ca_____ I please
have one of those and one of th_____?'

Poem 4
'Are you fr_____ at half past five?'
'Sorry, that's when my friends ar_____.'
'Then ho_____ ab_____ meeting at two or three?'
'Sorry, I'm bu_____.' 'When are you fr_____?'

B ▶ RC1.2 Listen and check. Then listen and repeat.

LISTENING

6A ▶ RC1.3 Listen to the conversation at a hotel reception. Circle the correct picture of the lost item.

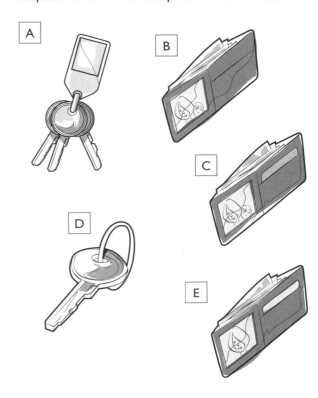

A   B   C   D   E

B Listen again and complete the lost property report.

AIRPORT HOTEL
LOST AND FOUND PROPERTY REPORT

Receptionist: *Angela West*

Guest: 1_____

Room number: 2_____

Mobile phone number: 3_____

Item lost:

4_____ with 5$ _____,

6_____ card and 7_____

Item checked and returned: ☐

Signature: *V Moretti*

Date: 8_____

21

TEST

Circle the correct option to complete the sentences.

1 A: Are _____ your keys on that table?
   B: No, I think they're Franco's.
   a) those   b) these   c) this

2 When _____ work?
   a) you finish   b) you do finish c) do you finish

3 A: Are you from Canada?
   B: No, I'm _____
   a) Mexicish   b) Mexican   c) Mexico

4 My parents _____ out on Fridays.
   a) go often   b) often go   c) often are

5 A: What's the time?
   B: It's _____.
   a) a quarter eleven
   b) half to five   c) eight fifteen

6 David's a _____ child. He never smiles.
   a) serious   b) funny   c) unfriendly

7 A: Is your name Chung?
   B: Yes, _____.
   a) I am   b) it is   c) my name is

8 A: Can you help us?
   B: Sorry, I _____ time.
   a) haven't got   b) don't have got c) hasn't got

9 A: What do you do in the evenings?
   B: I go to the cinema _____ I do nothing.
   a) or   b) and   c) but

10 A: What's that?
   B: It's a birthday card for my _____. He's four today.
   a) niece   b) uncle   c) nephew

11 _____ at the health centre?
   a) Jason does work
   b) Does Jason work   c) Works Jason

12 A: Is Carlos married?
   B: _____.
   a) No, he not   b) No, he isn't
   c) He's no married

13 My _____ is in the office.
   a) dairy   b) diery   c) diary

14 _____ a sandwich, please?
   a) Can I have   b) Could I   c) Do you

15 Eva _____ her MP3 player everywhere.
   a) listens to   b) listen to   c) listens

16 A: Susan, _____ is Julio.
   B: Hi, Susan. Nice to meet you.
   a) this   b) he   c) here

17 Paolo _____ dogs.
   a) no likes   b) don't like   c) doesn't like

18 How about _____ to the cinema?
   a) go   b) going   c) we go

19 They _____ a lot of sport.
   a) do   b) make   c) take

20 Ricardo _____ twenty-five.
   a) is   b) has got   c) have

21 A: Where are Kris and Marta?
   B: _____ in the café.
   a) There   b) Their   c) They're

22 You're very _____ today. Are you OK?
   a) quite   b) quiet   c) happy

23 A: Is this your pen?
   B: No, I think it's _____.
   a) Elena   b) Elena's   c) mine

24 A: How often do you go to a concert?
   B: _____.
   a) One a month.
   b) One in a month.   c) Once a month.

25 A: Do you like films?
   B: _____.
   a) Yes, I like   b) No, I don't like c) Yes, I do

26 I'm not Sylvie's father, I'm her brother! She's my _____!
   a) daughter   b) aunt   c) sister

27 Michelle, _____ free tonight?
   a) are you   b) do you   c) you are

28 I _____ go to the cinema – maybe once a year.
   a) never   b) hardly ever   c) sometimes

29 _____ a computer?
   a) Has Ian got   b) Ian has got   c) Has got Ian

30 That isn't your book. It's _____.
   a) my   b) Ana   c) mine

TEST RESULT **/30**

VOCABULARY rooms/furniture

1A Find ten rooms/furniture in the puzzle.

L	I	V	I	N	G	R	O	O	M	Z
C	W	L	N	O	I	N	A	G	E	R
U	A	K	I	T	C	H	E	N	M	I
P	R	Q	U	G	B	A	T	E	R	O
B	D	I	S	H	E	L	V	E	S	T
O	R	E	Y	B	D	E	A	T	O	H
A	O	Z	R	M	R	U	K	P	F	E
R	B	A	L	C	O	N	Y	Q	A	V
D	E	A	T	C	O	D	E	S	K	T
P	O	E	A	R	M	C	H	A	I	R

B Write the words in the correct group.

Places in a house	Furniture
living room	

GRAMMAR *there is/are*

ROOM FOR RENT

One bedroom for rent in a large flat with other students.

Good location – only ten minutes from the station.

Rent: €400 per month

Phone: Eduardo on 0427 392 28409

2A Read the advert and complete the conversation with the correct form of *there is/are*.

A: Hi, Eduardo, my name's Ken. I'm interested in the flat. Can I ask you some questions?

B: Sure.

A: ¹ *Is there*　 a living room?

B: No, ²_____ but ³_____ a big kitchen. We use it as a living room.

A: And ⁴_____ a television?

B: We've got a small TV in the kitchen and ⁵_____ an internet connection in each room.

A: Oh, that's good. So at the moment how many people ⁶_____ in the flat?

B: ⁷_____ two of us, me and Karol. Karol's Polish and I'm from Argentina. ⁸_____ anything else you want to know?

A: Er ... oh yes, are you near the shops?

B: Well, ⁹_____ about five or six shops near the station and ¹⁰_____ a large shopping centre about ten minutes away.

A: OK, thanks. It sounds great!

B Underline the key word with the main stress in each sentence.

1 Is there a <u>living</u> room?

2 There's a big kitchen.

3 Is there a television?

4 How many people are there?

5 There are two of us.

6 There's a large shopping centre.

C ▶ 4.1 Listen and check. Then listen and repeat.

VOCABULARY prepositions (1)

3 Underline the correct alternative.

1 A: Where's Antonia?
   B: She's *on* / *in* / *behind* her bedroom.

2 A: I want to take a photo of everyone.
   B: OK. Samad, could you stand *on* / *under* / *in front of* Tomas?

3 A: Where's your flat?
   B: It's *on* / *between* / *above* that shop.

4 A: Is there a café near here?
   B: Yes, there's one *between* / *on* / *in* the cinema and the post office.

5 A: Have you got today's newspaper?
   B: Yes. it's *in* / *on* / *between* the kitchen table.

6 Always look *behind* / *above* / *next to* you when you start your car.

7 A: Who's that *next to* / *between* / *in* your dad in the photo?
   B: That's my brother, Stefano.

8 A: Where's the cat?
   B: Look *under* / *above* / *between* the sofa.

READING

4A Label the picture with the words in the box.

~~wallpaper~~ mirror curtain sofa picture

1 *wallpaper*

2 _____

3 _____

4 _____

5 _____

B What do you think? Underline the alternatives in sentences 1–6.

In a small room ...

1 *have / don't have* lots of small furniture.

2 *use / don't use* one or two pieces of large furniture.

3 *have / don't have* a lot of pictures.

4 *put / don't put* a mirror on the wall.

5 *open / don't open* curtains in the day.

6 *paint / don't paint* your walls a dark colour.

C Read *Top tips for small rooms* and check your answers.

D Look at the photo in Exercise 4A. Complete the sentences with *There's/ There are.*

1 *There are* no armchairs.

2 _____ a big sofa next to the window.

3 _____ a picture on the wall.

4 _____ a curtain.

5 _____ a big mirror above the sofa.

6 _____ no lamps in the room.

7 _____ two tables in the room.

8 _____ a cup on the table.

9 _____ no shelves.

10 _____ a plant between the sofa and the window.

TOP TIPS FOR SMALL ROOMS
BY INTERIOR DESIGNER MARIA WRIGHT

In a small home it's important to choose the right furniture. With the wrong furniture, your room can look crowded but with the right furniture it can look spacious* and large.

People with small rooms usually make a big mistake. They put lots of furniture in the room — they often have two or three small armchairs and tables, or a table and a desk — and they put lots of small pictures on the walls.

A small room looks good with one or two big pieces of furniture, for example a sofa or a table — for relaxing, eating and working. Have one or two pictures, no more, and put up a mirror. A mirror in the right place gives more light and makes the room look big. Windows are very important because they make a room look light and spacious. Use curtains but don't close them in the day. Put wallpaper on one wall and paint the other walls a light colour, for example white or yellow; don't use brown or black or other dark colours.

*spacious = has a lot of space

WRITING punctuation

5A Add four full stops, three commas and four capital letters to the text.

a man lives on the twelfth floor of a tall building every morning he leaves home takes the lift down to the lobby and leaves the building in the evening he gets into the lift goes to the tenth floor opens the lift doors and walks up the stairs to his flat sometimes there's someone else in the lift and he goes up to the twelfth floor

B Why does the man do this?

LISTENING

1A Look at the photo of Pueblo Inglés and underline one alternative.

1 Pueblo Inglés is in *Spain / Canada / England*.

2 You can speak *French / English / Spanish* in Pueblo Inglés.

B ▶ 4.2 Listen and check.

C Listen again and underline the correct alternative.

1 English speakers pay *300 euros / <u>nothing</u>* to stay in Pueblo Inglés.

2 There are *twenty / forty* people in the village.

3 The people are all from *Spain and Australia / many different countries*.

4 People in Pueblo Inglés are all *in their twenties / between twenty and sixty years old*.

5 Every day Janet speaks English to *one Spanish student / different Spanish students*.

6 In the evening Janet *is free / eats with the Spanish students*.

7 The people in the village *sometimes / never* speak Spanish.

8 Janet *thinks it's hard work / likes it a lot*.

Pueblo Inglés

VOCABULARY places in a town

2 Where do you go? Complete the crossword with shops and places.

3 across: P H A R M A C Y

Across

3 You need some aspirin.

4 You like doing exercise.

6 You like looking at very old objects.

8 You need some money.

9 You want to watch a film.

Down

1 You want to watch a play.

2 You need some food for the weekend.

3 You want to buy a stamp and send a letter.

5 You want to see the mayor.

7 You want to do some English classes.

GRAMMAR can for possibility

3 Complete the conversations with the correct form of *can* and the subject in brackets.

Conversation 1

A: Hello. ¹ *Can I*_____ (I) change a hundred euros into rupiahs, please? For Indonesia.

B: Yes, ²_____ (you) but we haven't got any here at the moment. ³_____ (we) get them here in two or three days. ⁴_____ (you) collect them on Friday morning?

A: Friday's difficult – ⁵_____ (I / not) do it then. How about Saturday?

B: Sorry. We're closed on Saturday but ⁶_____ (you) collect them on Monday, if that's OK.

A: Yes, no problem.

Conversation 2

A: Hello. Welcome to Plainfield Sports Centre. ⁷_____ (I) help you?

B: Yes. My son wants extra swimming lessons. Have you got classes for beginners?

A: Er ... what time of day ⁸_____ (he) come?

B: He's at school until four so ⁹_____ (he) come in the evenings.

A: OK. We've got a class on Mondays.

B: Oh, ¹⁰_____ (he / not) come then. His favourite TV programme is on Mondays.

A: I see. ¹¹_____ (he) come on Thursday?

B: No, ¹²_____ (he / not). He always watches his other ...

A: ... favourite TV programme?

B: That's right!

4A Complete the quiz questions with verbs in the box.

~~eat~~ watch travel speak see

WHERE IN THE WORLD ... ?

1 Where can you _eat_ mooncake?
   a) Mexico   b) China   c) Sweden

2 Where can you _____ four languages in one country?
   a) Switzerland b) Canada c) Japan

3 Where can you _____ Michelangelo's famous statue of David?
   a) Brazil   b) Spain   c) Italy

4 Where can you _____ across eleven time zones in one country?
   a) Russia   b) the USA c) India

5 Where can you _____ sixteen different football teams in one city?
   a) Madrid   b) London
   c) Rio de Janeiro

B Circle the correct answers in the quiz.

C Read sentences 1–5 and check your answers.

1 Mooncake is a very sweet cake. You ⸦can⸧ eat it in China at the Mid-Autumn Festival.

2 In Canada you hear two languages, French and English, but in Switzerland there are four official languages: Italian, French, German and Romansch.

3 The statue of David is in Italy. You visit it in Florence.

4 India has got one time zone, the USA has four, and in Russia you go through eleven time zones.

5 Rio and Madrid have got a lot of football teams, but in London you choose between sixteen different football clubs including Arsenal, Chelsea and West Ham United.

D Look at Exercise 4C again. Add *can* to each sentence.

VOCABULARY prepositions (2)

5A Read sentences 1–7 and label the basketball players in the picture below.
1 Eduardo is in front of Dirk.
2 Andrei is opposite Eduardo.
3 Steve is on the right of Dirk.
4 Theo is behind Steve.
5 Tony is next to Andrei.
6 Neně is on the left of Tony.
7 Jorge is opposite Neně.

B Underline the correct alternative.
1 Andrei is *on the left of* / <u>*on the right of*</u> Tony.
2 Steve is *in front of* / *opposite* Theo.
3 Neně is *opposite* / *behind* Jorge.
4 Tony is *behind* / *next to* Neně.
5 Eduardo is *next to* / *on the left of* Jorge.
6 Andrei, Neně and Tony are *opposite* / *near* each other.

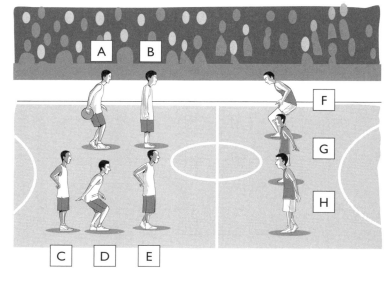

A _Dirk_   E _____
B _____   F _____
C _____   G _____
D _____   H _____

VOCABULARY things to buy

1A Write the shop names under pictures 1–10.

1 _sports shop_

2 _____

3 _____

4 _____

5 _____

6 _____

7 _____

8 _____

9 _____

10 _____

B Complete the things to buy from the shops.

1 Go to shop 1 to buy tra_iners____ or a swi_____
cos_____.

2 In shop 3 you can buy new_____ and
mag_____.

3 You can buy jea_____ and a jac_____ in shop 4.

4 Do you want an Italian-English dic_____? Go to
shop 9.

5 You can buy bre_____ and cak_____ in shop 5.

6 You go to shop 7 when you need a bla_____ DVD,
hea_____ or a mem_____ sti_____.

FUNCTION shopping

2 Add the words from the box to the conversations.

~~you~~ 'll Can in too got problem them
enough 're it expensive they

Conversation 1

A: Can you help me?

B: Yes?

A: Have you got these jeans black?

B: Black? I think so. Yes.

A: Oh, they aren't big. Have you got in size 16?

B: Er ... let me look. Ah, yes.

A: Great, I take them. How much are?

B: They £39.99.

Conversation 2

A: I help you?

B: Yes, we need a Scotland football shirt for Duncan.

A: OK. Try this one.

B: No, it's big. Have you it in small?

A: Here you are.

B: Thanks. That's great. How much is?

A: £60.

B: What? £60! That's too.

C: Mum!

B: No. No, thank you. Sorry, Duncan.

A: Fine. No.

LEARN TO say *no* politely in a shop

3 Put the words in the correct order to complete the
conversation.

Assistant: help / I / Can / you?
1 _Can I help you?_

Customer: thanks. / looking, / just / I'm
2 _____

Customer: you / Have / small? / in / this / T-shirt / got
3 _____

Assistant: No, / medium. / Only / sorry. / in
4 _____

Customer: No, / isn't / right. / it / anyway. / Thanks
5 _____

Assistant: red. / we've / in / it / got
6 _____

Customer: not / Mmm, I'm / think / I / sure. / to / need /
it. / about
7 _____

VOCABULARY food/drink

1A Complete the words.

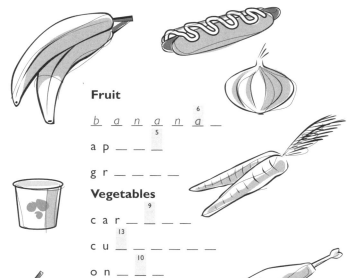

Fruit

_b_ _a_ _n_ _a_ _n_ _a_ (6)

a p _ _ _ _ (5)

g r _ _ _ _ _

Vegetables

c a r _ _ _ _ _ (9)

c u _ _ _ _ _ _ _ (13)

o n _ _ _ _ (10)

Meat and fish

c h _ _ _ _ _ (3)

s a _ _ _ _ _ _ (1)

h o _ _ d _ _ (8) (2)

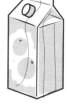

Drink

f r _ _ _ (12) j u _ _ _ _

w a _ _ _ (7)

_ _ l k (11)

Other

b r _ _ _

y _ g _ _ _ t (14)

b u _ _ _ r (4)

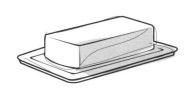

B Write the numbered letters from Exercise 1A to find the message.

_ _ _ , _ _ _a_ _ _ _ _ _ _ _ !
1 2 3 4 5 6 7 8 9 10 11 12 13 14

2A ▶ 5.1 Listen to the pronunciation. Are the underlined sounds the same (S) or different (D)?

1 m<u>i</u>lk   ch<u>i</u>cken   S
2 m<u>ea</u>t   br<u>ea</u>d
3 cuc<u>u</u>mber   <u>o</u>nion
4 s<u>au</u>sages   hot d<u>o</u>g
5 s<u>ar</u>dines   c<u>ar</u>rots
6 ban<u>a</u>na   gr<u>a</u>pe
7 yogh<u>ur</u>t   butt<u>er</u>
8 fr<u>ui</u>t   j<u>ui</u>ce

B Listen again and repeat.

GRAMMAR countable / uncountable nouns

3A Underline the correct alternative.

1 I drink _milk_ / _milks_ every day.
2 My parents eat a lot of _fruit_ / _fruits_.
3 We often have _roll_ / _rolls_ for breakfast.
4 I don't like _pea_ / _peas_.
5 I don't eat _meat_ / _meats_.
6 I really hate _rice_ / _rices_.
7 We hardly ever have _bean_ / _beans_.
8 There's a lot of _pasta_ / _pastas_ in my cupboard.

B Make the sentences above true for you.

1 _____
2 _____
3 _____
4 _____
5 _____
6 _____
7 _____
8 _____

4 Use the prompts below to write sentences. Make the nouns plural where necessary.

1 Apple / good / for you.
  Apples are good for you.
2 coffee / good / for you?
  _____
3 There / a lot of / sugar / the cupboard.
  _____
4 There / a lot of / sausage / the fridge.
  _____
5 he / like / grape?
  _____
6 I / not like / butter.
  _____
7 you / eat / a lot of / biscuit?
  _____
8 We not / eat / a lot of / egg.
  _____

READING

5A Read the article and match recipes 1–3 with shopping lists A–C.

TOO BUSY TO EAT?

Do you have a busy lifestyle? When you come home from work, are you too tired to cook in the evenings? Here are three easy-to-make dishes from TV chef James Conway.

1 Eggs à la Provençale

A dish with a sophisticated name, but in fact it's very simple. Mix together three eggs, some tomato sauce, a small onion, and some salt and pepper. Put some oil in a frying pan and when it's hot, add the egg mixture. Stir it around and 'There you go!'

2 Pasta salad

This is a flexible dish, so you can eat it every day. Mix together some cooked pasta – I like three-colour pasta – and two types of cooked vegetables (e.g. broccoli, tomatoes, corn on the cob, green peppers). Add some oil and chilli sauce, stir it around ... and enjoy!

3 Cola chicken

Cola chicken is simple to make. You need a chicken, some cola, an onion and a green pepper. Cut up the chicken, the onion, and the green pepper and put them together in a pan. Add some cola, some herbs and spices, and cover it with aluminium foil. Bake it at 350 degrees for one hour.

A SHOPPING LIST
pasta (3-colour)
tomatoes
broccoli
chilli sauce
oil

B SHOPPING LIST
eggs
tomato sauce
1 onion
salt
oil

C SHOPPING LIST
chicken
cola
green pepper
herbs and spices

B Which two shopping lists are not complete? Read the recipes again and add the missing ingredients to the lists.

GRAMMAR nouns with *a/an*, *some, any*

6 Complete the sentences with *a/an*, *some* or *any*.

1 Pasta salad hasn't got _any_ meat in it, but it's got _____ vegetables.
2 A: Are there _____ vegetables in Cola chicken?
   B: Yes, it's got _____ onion and _____ green pepper.
3 There isn't _____ chilli sauce in Eggs à la Provençale, but there's _____ tomato sauce.
4 Two dishes have got _____ oil in them and one hasn't got _____.
5 A: Is there _____ salt and pepper in the Pasta salad?
   B: No there isn't, but there's _____ hot sauce.
6 Cola chicken is _____ very simple dish.

7 Write sentences with *there's/there are* and *some/any*.

1 ✓ fruit   ✗ vegetables
   There's some fruit, but there aren't any vegetables.
2 ✓ bread   ✗ butter
3 ✗ fruit juice   ✓ water
4 ✗ bananas   ✓ apples
5 ✓ grapes   ✗ cheese
6 ✓ pasta   ✗ tomato sauce
7 ✗ onions   ✓ carrots
8 ✓ salt   ✗ pepper

VOCABULARY containers

1 Vic and Bob are going on a camping trip. Complete their conversation with eight of the words in the box. Make them plural if necessary.

> ~~can/tin~~ bottle bag cup packet
> jar tube mug carton bar roll

Bob: OK, Vic. Is everything here?

Vic: Yes, I think so.

Bob: OK. Three ¹ *cans*   of baked beans?

Vic: Yes.

Bob: Five ²_____ of chocolate?

Vic: Er ... yes.

Bob: One ³_____ of toothpaste?

Vic: Yeah.

Bob: Five ⁴_____ of water?

Vic: Right.

Bob: A ⁵_____ of cigarettes?

Vic: Bob, this is a no smoking holiday!

Bob: OK, OK. A ⁶_____ of jam?

Vic: Yes.

Bob: Ten ⁷_____ of sweets?

Vic: Bob, you're on a diet!

Bob: But they're sugar-free sweets.

Vic: Huh!

Bob: Two ⁸_____ of toilet paper?

Vic: Er ... toilet paper? Oh, no!!

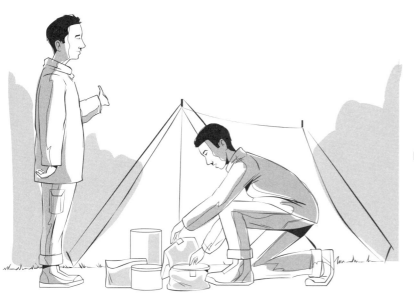

VOCABULARY large numbers

2A Write the numbers in words.

1 2,523   *two thousand, five hundred and twenty-three*
2 3,145   _____
3 1,101   _____
4 10,000   _____
5 721   _____
6 250,000 _____

B ▶ 5.2 Listen and check. Then listen and repeat.

GRAMMAR how much/many

3A Make questions with *how much/many* and a word/phrase from columns A and B. Make the nouns in column A plural if necessary.

A	B
1 ~~child~~	is there in a hamburger?
2 letter	are there in a mile?
3 beef	are there in English?
4 vowel	are there in the UK?
5 cent	is there in a 25-metre swimming pool?
6 water	are there in the English alphabet?
7 juice	is there in one can of cola?
8 sugar	~~are there in the average American family?~~
9 country	are there in a euro?
10 kilometres	is there in ten kilos of oranges?

1 *How many children are there in the average American family?*
2 _____
3 _____
4 _____
5 _____
6 _____
7 _____
8 _____
9 _____
10 _____

B Match answers a)–j) with questions 1–10.

a) 100   5
b) 375,000 litres
c) 1.61
d) two
e) 40 grams, or 10 spoons
f) twenty-six
g) four: England, Scotland, Wales and Northern Ireland
h) five
i) about 3.5 litres
j) 114 grams – one kilo makes eight burgers

LISTENING

4A ▶ **5.3 Listen to a radio programme and tick the best answer.**

On the junk food lover's diet ...

1 you can eat a lot of junk food.

2 you can eat a little junk food.

3 you can't eat any junk food.

B Complete the questions with *How much/ many.*

1 *How many*_____ hot dogs can you eat in a week?

2 _____ chocolate can you eat in a week?

3 _____ pieces of pizza can you eat in a week?

4 _____ packets of crisps can you eat in a week?

5 _____ hamburgers can you eat in a week?

6 _____ cola can you drink in a week?

C Listen again and answer questions 1–6.

GRAMMAR quantifiers

5 Make sentence b) the opposite of sentence a). Use the quantifiers in the box.

quite a lot (of)   a lot (of)   much   many   none   no

1 a) I don't drink very much coffee.

   b) I drink *quite a lot of* coffee.

2 a) I've got a lot of friends.

   b) I haven't got _____ friends.

3 a) There's a lot of pasta in the jar.

   b) There isn't _____ pasta in the jar.

4 a) I haven't got much time to relax.

   b) I've got _____ time to relax.

5 a) There are some tomatoes in the fridge.

   b) There are _____ tomatoes in the fridge.

6 a) Stamps? Yes, there are some here.

   b) Stamps? No, there are _____ here.

WRITING paragraphs

6A Read the blog and number the topics below in the correct order. The writer doesn't give information about two topics.

drinks

snacks

fast food

breakfast   1

foreign food

dinner

lunch

HOW MY FAMILY EATS

Hungarians love eating! We have four meals a day: breakfast, lunch, a snack and dinner. My son doesn't eat breakfast at home because he doesn't want to get up early. I make breakfast for him and he takes it to school. My husband and I eat breakfast at home. We like eating rolls with butter or cheese and ham or different kinds of salami. We don't usually have cereal with milk.

We have lunch when my son comes back from school – between 1p.m. and 2p.m. – and the whole family eats together. Lunch is the main meal of the day for us. I cook all day and we always eat hot food. We often have vegetable soup, and then we have the main dish – for example, pasta, cheese or meat with potatoes, rice or noodles.

We sometimes eat an afternoon snack – maybe some bread and fruit. My son likes having crisps for a snack but they aren't good for him.

We have dinner between 6p.m. and 7p.m. We eat something light or we have leftovers from lunch. We eat together and talk about our day. I like hearing my son talk about school. Our dinner is very relaxed.

We like food from other countries too, especially Italian food. We often eat pizza or spaghetti with bolognese sauce. We sometimes go to an Italian restaurant and I learn new dishes.

B Write four or five paragraphs about how your family eats. Write 80–100 words.

VOCABULARY restaurant words

1 Complete the article. Use each word <u>twice</u>.

> menu chef dishes bill order tip waiter

THE AMERICAN DINER

The American diner is a great place to eat but it's strange for foreigners. When you sit down, someone brings you a glass of ice water – you don't ¹ <u>order</u> the water, it just comes. The ²_____ is not a simple list of food, but it's a long list with hundreds of ³_____. A ⁴_____ in a diner can cook <u>anything</u> and everything! Luckily, there are often pictures of some of the ⁵_____ in the ⁶_____ to help you choose. When you ⁷_____ a simple sandwich, the ⁸_____ asks you lots of questions – what sort of bread, if you want cheese on it, etc. He writes all the information down and gives it to the ⁹_____.
At the end of the meal, you ask for the ¹⁰_____.
Usually, you leave the money on the table with the ¹¹_____ and you leave a ¹²_____ of 15–20%.
It's important to leave a ¹³_____ – in the USA, a ¹⁴_____ doesn't get much money!

FUNCTION ordering in a restaurant

2 Put the words in the correct order.

Waiter: ready / you / order / to / are?
¹ *Are you ready to order?*

Customer: soup, / like / I'd / onion / please / some
2 _____

Waiter: like / a / you / would / course / main?
3 _____

Customer: some / could / lamb / I / roast / have?
4 _____

Waiter: you / would / like / what / vegetables?
5 _____

Customer: I / and / have / please / potatoes / peas, / can?
6 _____

Waiter: drink / something / to?
7 _____

Customer: I / some / mineral / have / could / water?
8 _____

LEARN TO understand fast speech

3A ▶ 5.4 Listen and tick what the customers order.

	Customer 1	Customer 2	Customer 3
hamburger			
roll			
veggie burger			
lettuce			
onion			
tomato			
corn on the cob			
salad			

B Look at the phrases from Exercise 3A and draw lines to show the linking.

1 and‿a salad too, please
2 corn on the cob
3 and some onions on the burger
4 a hamburger in a roll
5 with onion and tomato
6 with lettuce and onion

C ▶ 5.5 Listen and check. Then listen and repeat.

VOCABULARY cooking

4 Complete the words about food and cooking with the letters from the alphabet (A–Z). Use each letter only once.

1 s <u>w</u> e e t
2 s a _ t
3 t o s _ i r
4 s p i _ e s
5 _ r e a _ f a s t
6 _ u _ c e
7 t o s _ u e e _ e
8 t o m i _
9 s o _ s a _ c e
10 t o t u r _ o _ e r
11 n o o _ l e _
12 _ a r k _ t
13 t o d _ o p
14 _ i l
15 v e _ e t _ b l e s
16 _ a n
17 _ i s _

f v d
l c t
b
s o
m k
h z u
  a
x w q
n g e
r p y j

GRAMMAR was/were

1 Complete the sentences with the correct form of *was/were*.

1 Jan and I _were_ in Paris at the weekend. It _was_ expensive, but interesting.

2 Simon and his wife _____ (not) at the theatre yesterday. They _____ at the cinema.

3 I _____ late, but the teacher _____ (not) angry.

4 Louise _____ sorry that you _____ (not) at her party.

5 We _____ in New York last summer and the people _____ very friendly.

6 The film _____ (not) funny, but the popcorn _____ really good!

2 Write the questions and short answers.

1 Paul Newman – actor? ✓ Canadian? ✗

   a) *Was Paul Newman an actor?*   *Yes, he was.*

   b) *Was he Canadian?*   *No, he wasn't.*

2 Beatrix Potter – writer? ✓ English? ✓

   a) _____   _____

   b) _____   _____

3 Beethoven and Wagner – dancers? ✗ German? ✓

   a) _____   _____

   b) _____   _____

4 Confucius – doctor? ✗ Chinese? ✓

   a) _____   _____

   b) _____   _____

5 Che Guevara and Eva Perón – singers? ✗ Argentinian? ✓

   a) _____   _____

   b) _____   _____

3 Complete the sentences with the correct form of *be* in the present or past.

1 Jan_'s_ quite talkative now, but he _wasn't_ (not) very talkative when he was a child.

2 There _____ a lot of people in the office yesterday afternoon, but there _____ only one person here now.

3 The weather _____ (not) very nice last weekend, but it _____ beautiful now.

4 My mother _____ retired now, but most of her life she _____ a teacher.

5 We _____ (not) at home yesterday, but we _____ here today.

6 The food here _____ fine last week, but this meal _____ (not) very good.

7 I _____ (not) very well yesterday and I _____ (not) well today.

8 Svetlana _____ at school with me when we were children and now she _____ a famous politician.

9 There _____ a lot of people at the concert last night, but there _____ (not) many here tonight.

10 I can see you _____ (not) very happy today. What's the matter? You _____ OK yesterday.

VOCABULARY dates and times

4A Write how you say the dates.

1 19/3/1959 *'March the nineteenth, nineteen fifty-nine' / 'The nineteenth of March, nineteen fifty-nine.'*

2 1/5/2010 _____
_____

3 31/3/2002 _____
_____

4 30/10/1995 _____
_____

5 26/1/2005 _____
_____

6 13/10/1957 _____
_____

7 21/5/1910 _____
_____

8 6/1/1805 _____
_____

B ▶ 6.1 Listen and tick the dates you hear in the list in Exercise 4A. Which one don't you hear?

5 Add *on*, *in*, *ago*, *yesterday* or *last* to each sentence. Some sentences have two correct answers.

                    on / last
1 It was very cold /Friday.

2 I was at university 1995.

3 He wasn't at home a week.

4 We were at the party weekend.

5 Were you at work Wednesday?

6 My parents were both eighty years old year.

7 The children were tired morning, and today, too.

8 It was cold July.

9 We were in the café afternoon.

10 Simon was here ten minutes, but he isn't here now.

READING

6A Read the article and tick the best title.

1 **Work and friendship don't mix**   2 **Film star romances**   3 **Famous friends**

Britney and Justin, Kate and Leonardo ... celebrities who have something in common: a close friendship.

Some film stars were friends when they were children. Americans Leonardo DiCaprio and Tobey McGuire (Spiderman) were good friends, starting when they were child actors looking for work on the same films and TV shows.

Work often brings famous people together. Justin Timberlake and Britney Spears were on the *Mickey Mouse Club Show*, a children's TV programme, together when they were eleven years old. George Clooney and Brad Pitt were co-stars in *Ocean's Eleven*, and are very close now.

Sometimes friends in real life play lovers on screen, and that can be difficult. Kate Winslet and Leonardo DiCaprio are good friends, but they don't have a romantic relationship. In the film *Titanic*, for both of them the kissing scenes were strange. 'It was like I was kissing my brother,' says Kate.

Of course there are stars who don't want to be friends with other stars. Hugh Grant says he doesn't like spending time with other actors. 'I don't have any actor friends,' Grant says, 'I'm friends on the film and then I walk away.'

B How do the stars know each other? Are they friends from childhood (C), friends from work (W), or doesn't the article say (?)? Tick the correct box. Sometimes two answers are possible.

	C	W	?
Leonardo and Tobey	✓		
Justin and Britney			
George and Brad			
Kate and Leonardo			

C Are the sentences true (T) or false (F)?

1 Leonardo and Tobey were on the same TV show together.   *F*
2 George and Brad are good friends.
3 Kate and Leonardo were real life lovers.
4 Kate doesn't think it was easy to be in a romantic film with Leonardo.
5 Hugh Grant has got a lot of actor friends.
6 He's unfriendly when he works with other actors.

D Complete the sentences with the words in the box. Then read the article again and check.

> away   with   together   on   for (x2)   in (x4)

1 The celebrities in the article all have something _____ common.
2 Leonardo and Tobey were child actors looking _____ work on the same films.
3 Work brings famous people _____.
4 George Clooney and Brad Pitt were co-stars _____ *Ocean's Eleven*.
5 Sometimes friends _____ real life play lovers on screen.
6 The kissing scenes _____ the film *Titanic* were strange _____ both Kate and Leonardo.
7 Hugh Grant doesn't want to be friends _____ other stars.
8 He says he's friends _____ the film and then he walks _____.

GRAMMAR past simple

1A Complete the life story of Anita Roddick. Use the past simple form of the verbs in the box.

> grow up   leave   open (×2)   die   meet   travel   sell
> come   have   go   work   get married   study

Anita Roddick started The Body Shop, the first 'green' cosmetics* company. She was born Anita Perelli in the UK in 1942 and [1] _grew up_____ in Littlehampton in the south of England. Her parents [2]_____ from Italy and she [3]_____ three brothers and sisters.

After she [4]_____ school, Anita [5]_____ to Bath College and [6]_____ to become a teacher. After college, she [7]_____ all around the world. Then she [8]_____ Gordon Roddick and they [9]_____ in 1970. Anita and Gordon [10]_____ a restaurant and then a hotel. At the same time Anita [11]_____ for the United Nations.

She [12]_____ the first Body Shop in Brighton, England, in 1976. The shop [13]_____ only fifteen items with only natural ingredients. It now sells over 300 items to 77 million customers and in 2004 was the twenty-eighth top name in the world of business. Anita Roddick [14]_____ in 2007.
She left behind a husband and two daughters.

*cosmetics = make-up, for example lipstick, mascara, hand cream

B Correct the information. Use the negative form of the verb.

1 Anita lived in Italy.
Anita didn't live in Italy.

2 She went to Bath University.
_____

3 She became a teacher.
_____

4 After college she stayed at home.
_____

5 She and her husband started a café.
_____

6 She had a son.
_____

2A How do you pronounce -ed in past simple verbs? Write the past simple form of the regular verbs below in the correct place in the table.

> work   change   love   play   finish   start   stop
> want   help   try   enjoy   travel   hate

/t/	/d/	/ɪd/
worked		

B ▶ 6.2 Listen and check. Then listen and repeat.

C Write the past simple of the irregular verbs below.

1	think	_thought_	7	know	_____
2	meet	_____	8	draw	_____
3	speak	_____	9	write	_____
4	grow	_____	10	sleep	_____
5	wake	_____	11	leave	_____
6	teach	_____	12	buy	_____

D ▶ 6.3 Listen to the vowel sound in the verbs. Write them in the correct place in the table.

/ɔː/	/e/
thought	
/əʊ/	/uː/

GRAMMAR past simple: questions

3 Write questions about Anita Roddick.

1 Where _did her parents come from?_____
Her parents came from Italy.

2 Where _____?
She grew up in Littlehampton.

3 How many _____?
She had three brothers and sisters.

4 What _____?
After school, she went to Bath College.

5 When _____?
She got married in 1970.

6 Where _____?
She opened the first Body Shop in Brighton.

7 When _____?
She died in 2007.

LISTENING

4A Read the information about Zsilan and Lin.
Then tick the correct box for sentences 1–5.

My name is Zsilan.
I was born in Beijing
on May 8th 1997.
My real parents
are dead, but an
Australian man and
woman adopted* me,
and now they are my
mummy and daddy.
Now I live in Sydney.

Zsilan   Lin

My name is Lin. My
birthday is May 8th.
I was born in Beijing.
I don't remember my
real parents, but now
I have Australian
parents and I live in
Melbourne.

*adopt = take into a new family

		True	Maybe
I	Zsilan and Lin are from China.		
2	They were born on the same day in the same year.		
3	Their Australian parents adopted* them.		
4	They live in different cities in Australia.		
5	They know each other.		

B ▶ 6.4 Listen and check.

C Listen again and underline the correct answer.
1 Philip and Denise adopted Zsilan in *1999*/*2005*.
2 They brought her home when she was about *one*/*two*.
3 At first, Zsilan was very *happy*/*unhappy*.
4 They put *letters*/*a photo* on the website.
5 Zsilan and Lin looked *the same*/*different*.
6 The girls met in *Sydney*/*Melbourne*.
7 They *loved*/*didn't like* each other from the first moment.
8 The girls *lived*/*didn't live* together.
9 They like dancing and *swimming*/*singing*.
10 They found out they were sisters when they were *eight*/*ten*.

D ▶ 6.5 Complete the sentences from the recording
with the words in the box. Then listen and check.

very (x2)   really   at first   a lot   about   much

Philip: She was, er, ¹_____ two years old, but
           ²_____ there was a problem …

Denise: Yes, she was a ³_____ intelligent little girl, but at
           first she was also ⁴ _____ quiet. She ate
           ⁵_____ … but she didn't talk ⁶_____ …
           we didn't know what to do.

Philip: Yes, she was ⁷_____ unhappy.

WRITING *because, so, and, but*

5 Join each sentence in 1–9 with *because, so, and* or
but. Then write a paragraph.
1 Kasia didn't study last night. She felt too tired.
2 She needed some fresh air. She went out for a walk.
3 It was a warm evening. There were a lot of people in the street.
4 They looked happy. They weren't very friendly.
5 She met an old friend. They went to a café.
6 They didn't talk very much. They were happy to be together again.
7 Kasia drank coffee; he didn't drink anything. He wasn't thirsty.
8 They wanted to meet again. He gave her his phone number.
9 Kasia tried the number. It didn't work. She isn't very happy now.

Kasia didn't study last night because she felt too tired. She
needed some fresh air …

_____
_____
_____
_____
_____
_____
_____
_____
_____
_____
_____
_____
_____

VOCABULARY weekend activities

1A Complete the poem with the past simple form of the verbs in the box.

go (×2)   watch (×2)   play (×2)   go for   stay (×2)

'I ¹_went____ shopping and ²_____ TV
then ³_____ some golf and ⁴_____ tea.'
'We ⁵_____ with friends in Amsterdam
and all ⁶_____ clubbing till 3a.m.'
'I ⁷_____ a DVD at home
and ⁸_____ the piano all alone.'
'Well my weekend was really great.
I ⁹_____ at home and cooked, and ate.'

B Read the poem aloud.

FUNCTION making conversation

2A Put the words in the correct order.

1 weekend / how / your / was?
   How was your weekend?

2 did / do / what / you?
   _____

3 did / what / see / film / you?
   _____

4 good / it / was?
   _____

5 with / go / you / who / did?
   _____

6 on / you / did / what / do / Sunday?
   _____

7 you / did / go / where?
   _____

8 music / was / how / the?
   _____

9 did / get / you / time / what / back?
   _____

10 now / tired / you / are?
   _____

B Match answers a)–j) with questions 1–10 above.
a) With my cousin, Ian.   *5*
b) Great! The bands were fantastic!
c) Well, on Saturday we went to the cinema.
d) Perfect!
e) The new Batman film.
f) To Hyde Park, in London.
g) On Sunday I went to a rock festival with Fran.
h) Yes, very good.
i) No, I feel fine.
j) After midnight.

3A Circle the best answer to show interest.

1 A: What did you do on Saturday?
   B: I had lunch with my grandparents.
   A: a) It was nice.   b) That sounds nice.

2 A: Did you have a good day yesterday?
   B: No, we went for a walk and it rained!
   A: a) Really? That sounds interesting.
      b) So what did you do?

3 A: Did you have a good weekend?
   B: I wasn't very well so I stayed in bed.
   A: a) That sounds awful.   b) It was terrible.

4 A: How was your weekend?
   B: Fantastic, thanks!
   A: a) Why, what did you do?
      b) Really? That sounds fantastic.

5 A: Did you do anything special at the weekend?
   B: No, we just stayed at home and relaxed.
   A: a) That sounds terrible.   b) That sounds lovely.

B ▶ 6.6 Listen to the conversations and read aloud at the same time.

LEARN TO keep a conversation going

4 Complete the conversation with phrases a)–i) below. Write the correct letter.
A: Hi, Jamala. How was your weekend?
B: OK, thanks.
A: Did you go to Gerhardt's jazz concert?
B: Yes, I did. ¹_h____.
A: Really? ²_____?
B: Well, no, there weren't ... ³_____.
A: That sounds bad! ⁴_____?
B: Gerhardt's mother and father, but ⁵_____.
A: That's good. ⁶_____?
B: No, I didn't. ⁷_____.
A: That's quite early. ⁸_____?
B: He was happy. ⁹_____.

a) they enjoyed it.
b) Did you get home late?
c) Who were the other people?
d) How did Gerhardt feel about it?
e) only me and two other people.
f) The concert ended at about ten o'clock.
g) Were there many people there?
h) ~~It was very good.~~
i) He loves playing, so it wasn't a problem for him.

REVIEW AND CHECK 2: UNITS 4–6

GRAMMAR past simple

1A Complete the forum entries with the correct form of the verbs in the box.

be (×5)   bring   buy (×2)   do   eat   go (×2)   have (×2)   play   see

Do you remember the 60s? ❋

Well, we ¹ _were_ a typical family. We
² _____ (not) poor ... We ³ _____ the
same kind of furniture as now. In the living room there
⁴ _____ armchairs, a sofa and a black and white
television. We ⁵ _____ our first colour TV in 1968.
Doris K

We ⁶ _____ (not) food at the supermarket and every
morning a man ⁷ _____ fresh milk, bread and eggs to
our house.   **Terry G**

After school, my friends and I ⁸ _____ to the corner shop
next to the post office. For ten pence we got five big bars of chocolate
and ⁹ _____ it all!   **John M**

There was so much new technology – there ¹⁰ _____
new machines in the kitchen and the garden, and new styles of cars.
I remember my first pocket calculator – it ¹¹ _____
amazing! Of course, we ¹² _____ (not) mobile phones or
home computers ... Life was nice and slow.   **Eloise B**

When I think of the 1960s I think of family. We always
¹³ _____ things together. We were a big family
with three of us boys and five girls. At the weekend we
¹⁴ _____ football or other games and we often
¹⁵ _____ for walks. Sometimes we went to the theatre in
town and ¹⁶ _____ a play. The important thing was that
we were together.   **Winston T**

B Complete the questions.
1 Doris and her family / poor?
   Were Doris and her family poor?
2 When / her family / buy / their first colour TV?
   _____
3 Terry's family / go shopping for food / at the supermarket?
   _____
4 Where / they / buy / milk / bread / eggs?
   _____
5 How much / chocolate / John and his friends / get / for ten pence?
   _____
6 How many / brothers and sisters / Winston / have?
   _____

C Write answers for questions 1–8 in Exercise 1B.
1 _No, they weren't._   4 _____
2 _____   5 _____
3 _____   6 _____

VOCABULARY revision

2A Look at the forum entries in Exercise 1A and find:
1 two rooms in a house
   living room, kitchen
   _____
2 two pieces of furniture
   _____
   _____
3 four electronic items
   _____
   _____
4 four weekend activities
   _____
   _____
5 four places in town
   _____
   _____

B Put the letters in order to make words and phrases. Start with the underlined letters.
a) iigdnn mroo   _dining room_
b) pobacurd   _____
c) sholoc   _____
d) remmoy ckits   _____
e) deeshaphon   _____
f) yats ni deb   _____
g) bedrawor   _____
h) og glibbunc   _____
i) ummsue   _____
j) trabomoh   _____

C Add words a)–j) to groups 1–5 in Exercise 2A.

3 Find twelve food words in the puzzle.

C	H	O	C	O	L	A	T	E
H	B	V	U	L	T	E	A	B
I	I	L	G	R	A	P	E	U
C	S	Y	O	G	H	U	R	T
K	C	M	X	C	R	B	B	T
E	U	I	V	D	Y	R	E	E
N	I	L	V	Z	L	E	A	R
Q	T	K	B	A	N	A	N	A
H	O	N	E	Y	M	D	N	N

38

GRAMMAR countable / uncountable nouns

4A Add *-s* where necessary to the food on the list.

> 2 kilos of orange<u>s</u>   1 tin of bean
>
> 1 kilo of apple   2 packets of pasta
>
> 1/2 kilo of cheese   3 cartons of milk
>
> 1 bag of rice   1 kilo of carrot

B Underline the correct alternatives in the phone call.

A: Hi, Jo. Where are you?

B: Hi. I'm at the supermarket. I left the shopping list at work. Can I check some things? [1]*How much / How many* fruit have we got?

A: Let me look. [2]*No / None.*

B: OK. [3]*How much / How many* vegetables [4]*is / are* there?

A: Lots, but we haven't got [5]*some / any* potatoes. And we need [6]*a / some* spaghetti. Maybe two packets?

B: Right. [7]*Is / Are* there [8]*a / any* water?

A: Yes, we've got [9]*a / some* bottle in the fridge, but we haven't got [10]*some / any* milk. Can you buy three cartons?

B: Sure. That's all, thanks. See you soon!

VOCABULARY prepositions (1) and (2)

5A Look at the picture. Tick four true sentences. Correct the false sentences.

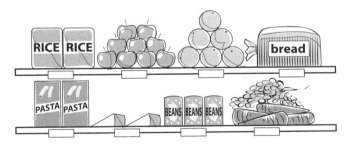

1 The oranges are next to the bread.

2 The cheese is between the beans and the carrots.

3 The pasta is behind the rice.

4 The apples are on the left of the oranges.

5 The grapes are in front of the carrots.

6 The bread is above the grapes and the carrots.

7 The apples are between the rice and the oranges.

8 The beans are on the right of the carrots.

_____

_____

_____

_____

B ▶ RC2.1 Listen and check.

VOCABULARY life story verbs

6A Complete the life story of a famous man. Use the past simple form.

He was [1]bo<u>rn</u>_____ in Germany in 1879. He [2]st_____ violin when he was very young, but he hated it. When he was fifteen, his father [3]lo_____ his job and the family [4]mo_____ to Italy. He wasn't a very good student, and at 16, he [5]le_____ Italy for Switzerland to finish his studies, and he [6]me_____ his future wife Mileva there. He [7]fi_____ his studies and two years later, he [8]fo_____ a job with the Swiss government. He and Mileva [9]go_____ married in 1903, and they [10]ha_____ three children. In 1911, he [11]be_____ a professor at the University of Zurich. He and his second wife, Elsa, [12]we_____ to America in 1932, and [13]bo_____ a house in New Jersey. His name was famous in the years after, in connection with atomic energy and the equation $E = MC^2$. He [14]di_____ in 1955.

B Who is the famous man?

FUNCTION shopping; ordering food

7A Put the words in the correct order.

1 At a clothes shop

  a) only / got / a / sorry, / we've / medium
     Sorry, we've only got a medium.

  b) help / can / you / I?
    _____

  c) small. / too / it's / anyway. / thanks
    _____

  d) large / a / in / got / this / you / have?
    _____

2 At a restaurant

  a) yes, / like / with / potatoes / rice / I'd / chicken / and / the
    _____
    _____

  b) would / what / like / drink / and / you / to?
    _____
    _____

  c) order / to / ready / you / are?
    _____
    _____

  d) I / can / glass / of / water, / have / please / a / mineral?
    _____

B Put the conversations above in the correct order.

1 At a clothes shop: <u>b</u> _ _ _

2 At a restaurant: _ _ _ _

TEST

Circle the correct option to complete the sentences.

1 _____ a balcony ?
  a) Has it   b) Is there   c) Are there

2 Yesterday we _____ in the Czech Republic.
  a) went   b) was   c) were

3 You can watch plays at the _____.
  a) theatre   b) sports centre   c) cinema

4 We've got _____ butter in the fridge.
  a) some   b) a   c) any

5 I _____ at home on Saturday.
  a) staid   b) staied   c) stayed

6 Jessie and Karl got married _____.
  a) two weeks ago   b) in two weeks   c) last two weeks

7 **A:** Can I help you?
  B: Thanks, I _____.
  a) just look   b) 'm just looking   c) just looking

8 We saw James _____.
  a) the last year   b) a year ago
  c) in 8th December

9 _____ go to work by bus?
  a) Cans she   b) Does she can   c) Can she

10 These jeans are _____ for me.
  a) too big   b) not enough big
  c) too much big

11 _____ tins of baked beans have we got?
  a) How much   b) Where   c) How many

12 Don't stand _____ the television, I can't see!
  a) behind   b) in front of   c) next to

13 We met _____ 2005.
  a) on   b) in   c) at

14 Where _____ at the weekend?
  a) you did go   b) did you go   c) did you went

15 Greg, _____ bread?
  a) are there any   b) is there a   c) is there any

16 How much _____ have we got?
  a) biscuits   b) toothpaste   c) baked beans

17 The letter D is _____ B in the alphabet.
  a) near   b) above   c) next to

18 _____ at the party last night?
  a) Was Victor   b) Were Victor   c) Victor was

19 **A:** Are you ready to order?
  B: Yes. _____ some chicken soup, please.
  a) Could I   b) I like   c) I'd like

20 We had a great holiday. I _____ to come home.
  a) no wanted   b) didn't wanted   c) didn't want

21 Would you like any _____?
  a) vegetables   b) vegatables   c) vegtables

22 **A:** Did you like the film?
  B: Yes, _____.
  a) I did like.   b) I did.   c) I liked.

23 _____ visit the museum in the evenings?
  a) Can you   b) You can   c) Do you can

24 Two _____ of coffee, please.
  a) mugs   b) rolls   c) tubes

25 There _____ cheese on the table.
  a) 's a   b) are some   c) 's some

26 I loved languages when I was at school, _____ I became an English teacher.
  a) so   b) because   c) then

27 How _____ do we need for the recipe?
  a) many fruit   b) many eggs   c) much apples

28 Kieron, can you stand _____ Stefan, please?
  a) on the right of   b) on left of   c) on the left

29 Do you like _____?
  a) sardine   b) sardines   c) a sardine

30 **A:** That jacket looks good on you.
  B: Thanks. I _____.
  a) have it   b) 'll take it
  c) 'm not sure about

TEST RESULT   /30

VOCABULARY travel

1A Rewrite the sentences using the words in the box. You do not need two of the words.

~~empty~~ noisy cheap boring uncomfortable slow expensive quiet fast comfortable crowded interesting

1 There were no visitors in the museum.
 The museum was _empty_ .

2 This bed's very hard – I can't relax on it.
 This bed's _____.

3 The train travels at 165 kilometres an hour.
 The train is very _____.

4 There were a lot of people on the beach.
 The beach was _____.

5 The book's good and has a lot of useful information.
 The book's _____.

6 The hotel is perfect – no cars outside, no children around, so I can sleep all day.
 The hotel is _____.

7 The car was $35,000 so he didn't buy it.
 The car was too _____ for him.

8 I didn't like the film. I slept for most of it.
 The film was _____.

9 These jeans didn't cost a lot.
 These jeans were quite _____.

10 I can't sleep because of the party in the flat below.
 The party is very _____.

B ▶ **7.1** Listen and repeat the adjectives from Exercise 1A.

C Listen again and write the adjectives in the correct place according to the stress.

1 O	2 Oo
cheap	*empty*
3 Ooo	**4 oOo**
5 oOoo	

GRAMMAR comparatives

2 Correct the mistakes in the sentences.

1 Hondas are popular than Suzukis.
 Hondas are more popular than Suzukis.

2 South Africa's hoter than Italy.
 _____

3 I'm more old than my brother.
 _____

4 Indian food is spicyer than English food.
 _____

5 Lena's intelligenter than me.
 _____

6 Cola is sweetter than lemonade.
 _____

7 Chinese is more difficult that English.
 _____

8 Crisps are badder for you than chips.
 _____

3 Complete the article with the comparative form of the adjectives in brackets.

Either ... or...?

We ask singer and actress Sonia Haig to choose. Which is better ... ?

Q: Singing or acting?
A: Singing. Singing is [1] _easier_ (easy) for me than acting.

Q: Healthy food or junk food?
A: Junk food. I know healthy food is [2]_____ (good) for me, but after a concert all I want is a pizza or a hamburger and chocolate!

Q: Relaxing on a beach or visiting an art gallery?
A: Oh, visiting an art gallery because it's [3]_____ (interesting). Sitting on a beach is boring.

Q: Dinner at a restaurant or dinner at home?
A: That's a difficult question. I like cooking, but I like having dinner at a restaurant because it's [4]_____ (romantic) than eating at home.

Q: Family or friends?
A: Family. I'm [5]_____ (close) to my sister than to my friends and I phone my parents every day.

Q: Summer or winter?
A: Well, I love looking at snow ... but winter is [6]_____ (cold) and I prefer being hot. OK, summer.

Q: New York or Paris?
A: I love Paris, but I love New York more because it's [7]_____ (big) than Paris and I like all the shops. I have an apartment near Central Park.

Q: Cats or dogs?
A: Dogs. They're [8]_____ (friendly) than cats!

READING

4A Read the emails. Are Tim and Mike good travel partners?

Hi Dan,

Mike and I arrived in Barcelona on Saturday. The first night we were in a self-catering apartment near the beach. I didn't sleep well because it was too noisy, so yesterday I moved to a hotel in the city centre. Mike stayed at the apartment because it's quite cheap. My hotel's very comfortable and quiet and it's got Spanish TV, so I can practise my Spanish in the evenings.

Yesterday Mike came with me to the Picasso Museum. I thought it was fantastic, but he wanted to leave after an hour. He said it was boring, so we went to the beach and met some local people and he talked to them for almost three hours ... that was boring! Of course, he spoke in English because he doesn't know much Spanish.

Last night I wanted to go to a restaurant to try the local food, but Mike said it was too expensive. We went to a cheap snack bar and the food was awful.

Hope you're well.

Tim

Hi Lucy,

Tim and I are here in beautiful Barcelona. I'm in a self-catering apartment near the beach. It's not very comfortable, but I only go there to sleep. The first night there was a party next door and I danced until 3a.m. Tim said it was too noisy and he moved into a hotel in the city centre. He stays in his room in the evenings and watches TV! Can you believe it – watching TV on holiday!?

Yesterday we went to the Picasso Museum. Well, it was OK ... for about an hour ... but Tim wanted to stay there all day! You know me ... I like relaxing on the beach and meeting people – yesterday I met some great people from Madrid and we chatted all afternoon.

Tim always wants to eat in expensive places, but I like buying food from shops and eating it on the beach. Last night we went to a snack bar. The food was terrible.

Mike

B Who do you think says sentences 1–8? Write Tim (T), Mike (M) or both (TM).

1 I haven't got much money.   *M*
2 A good night's sleep is important for me.
3 When I visit another country I try to learn some of the language.
4 We don't enjoy the same things.
5 I love going to art galleries and museums.
6 I talked to some Spanish people on the beach yesterday.
7 I don't like eating expensive food.
8 The food in the snack bar wasn't good.

C Read the emails again and answer the questions.

1 Which is more expensive: the apartment or the hotel?
   the hotel

2 Which is further from the city centre: the apartment or the hotel?
   _____

3 Which is noisier in the evenings: the apartment or the hotel?
   _____

4 Which is more comfortable: the apartment or the hotel?
   _____

5 Who is more talkative: Tim or Mike?
   _____

6 Who is more serious: Tim or Mike?
   _____

7 Who is better at speaking Spanish: Tim or Mike?
   _____

8 Who is more laid back: Tim or Mike?
   _____

VOCABULARY places (1)

1 Complete the puzzle and find what you have when y
go on holiday.

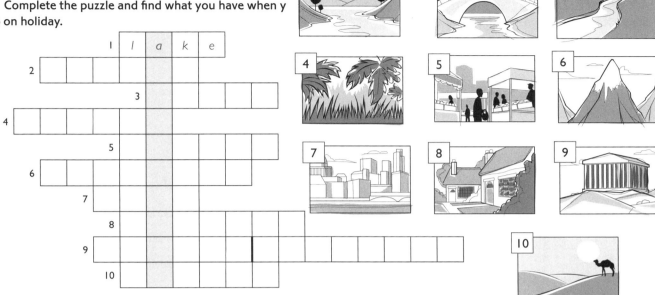

```
  1      l  a  k  e
2 [ ][ ][ ]
        3 [ ][ ][ ][ ][ ][ ][ ]
4 [ ][ ][ ][ ][ ]
     5 [ ][ ][ ][ ][ ]
6 [ ][ ][ ][ ]
   7 [ ][ ][ ]
      8 [ ][ ][ ][ ][ ][ ][ ]
   9 [ ][ ][ ][ ][ ][ ][ ][ ][ ][ ]
     10 [ ][ ][ ][ ][ ]
```

You have _____!

GRAMMAR superlatives

2A Read adverts A–C. Which holiday is good for:

1 a family?
2 people who like relaxing?
3 people who like active holidays?

A

LUXURY WEEKEND
A relaxing weekend at the beautiful 5-star
Hanover Hotel. Swim in the warm sea and
relax on the beach all day! Tennis courts
and bicycles are available. The perfect
laid-back holiday.

(3 nights – €1,490 per person)

B

MOUNTAIN ADVENTURE
Mountain biking in
the Indian Himalayas
– spend the day
biking and sleep in
tents at night. Prepare
for temperatures
of –10°C! A real
adventure for the
sporty holidaymaker.

(10 days – €2,490
per person)

C

FAMILY FUN
Camp Family has
everything your children
need to have a good time
– a lovely blue lake, an
adventure playground,
mini-golf and go-karts.
Stay in a self-catering
apartment. Sit back,
relax and let us give your
children the holiday of a
lifetime!

(6 days – €990 per family)

B Write sentences about the holidays using the
superlative of the adjective.

1 expensive   *The most expensive is Mountain adventure.*
2 cheap   _____
3 comfortable   _____
4 noisy   _____
5 long   _____
6 easy   _____
7 difficult   _____
8 short   _____
9 uncomfortable   _____
10 cold   _____

3A Write the questions.

1 What / long / word in this sentence?
   What's the longest word in this sentence?

2 What / short / word on this page?
   _____

3 Which / interesting / text in units 1–6 of this book?
   _____

4 Which / good / exercise on this page?
   _____

5 What / difficult / grammar point in English?
   _____

6 Who / happy / person in your family?
   _____

7 Who / friendly / person in your English class?
   _____

8 Which / bad / restaurant in town?
   _____

B Answer the questions in Exercise 3A.

43

LISTENING

4A ▶ 7.2 **Look at the map and listen to Nick's audio diary. Does his train go to or from Moscow?**

B Read sentences 1–8 below and check any new words in your dictionary.

1 The Trans-Siberian train journey takes nine days. *F*

2 The compartment is for two people.

3 Anton doesn't speak much English.

4 Nick can see snow, forests, villages, and lakes out of the window.

5 Nick and Anton buy food from women on the train.

6 They drink a lot of coffee on the train.

7 On the last evening of the journey, Nick went to a party.

8 Nick loved the Trans-Siberian train journey.

C Listen to Nick's diary again. Are sentences 1–8 true (T) or false (F)?

D Correct the false sentences.

1 The Trans-Siberian train journey takes seven days.

_____

_____

_____

_____

_____

_____

_____

WRITING checking and correcting

5A Read the extracts from Nick's blog. Underline and correct ten more mistakes. Check:

- the spelling
- past tense forms
- singular and plural

Hi, it's Nick again. We started the day with a surprise – but not a good one. Anton and I ~~goed~~ *went* to the dining car for brekfast and there wasn't any food. That wasn't a big problem because I had some biscuit and we drinked some tea, but then we went back for lunch and it was the same situation. The waiter told us that there's a station where they usually get food, but the food truck wasn't there.

Nobody on the train was worried about this becaus almost everybody broght their own food. A guy called Egor gaves us half of his roast chicken and a Chinese couple gave us some bread. Peoples were so kind. Anton and I talked about how to thank them ... so I tought them some English songs and it were really just a big party. My best day on the train!

B Write a short text about one day on a journey. It can be a real journey or an imaginary one. Write 80–100 words. Use the questions to help you.

- Where were you?
- How did you travel?
- What happened?
- Was it a good day?

C Check and correct any mistakes.

VOCABULARY places (2)

1 Add the missing vowels to make places in towns.

1 sq___r_
2 c__r p__rk
3 sw__mm__ng p___l
4 th___tr_
5 l__br__ry
6 b__s st__t___n
7 __rt g__ll__ry
8 t___r__st __nf__rm__t___n
9 p__rk
10 m__s___m

FUNCTION giving directions

2 Look at the map of Dublin, Ireland, and complete the conversation. Speaker A is at Pearse Street station (START) and wants to go to the Tourist Information Office (TI).

A: Excuse me. Can you tell me the ¹ _way_ to the Tourist Information Office, please?

B: Sure. Go down here and ² _____ right into Lincoln Place and then right again into Nassau Street.

A: OK.

B: Then go ³ _____ on down Nassau Street. Go ⁴ _____ Kildare Street and ⁵ _____ Street.

A: OK, so I stay on Nassau Street.

B: Yes, until the end but then don't turn right ⁶ _____ Grafton Street.

A: Not Grafton Street, OK.

B: Go straight ⁷ _____, into a small street ... I forget the name ... and the Tourist Information Office is on the ⁸ _____.

A: Great. Thank you!

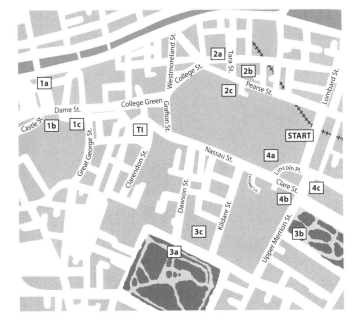

3 Read the information and look at the map. Circle the correct number of the destination.

Walking tours of Dublin

1 To Dublin Castle
From the Tourist Information Office, go to College Green and turn left. Go down College Green and Dame Street, and turn left into Castle Street. It's on the left and number 1a / (1b) / 1c on your map.

2 From Dublin Castle to Trinity College
Go back to Dame Street and into College Green and then left into College Street. Turn right into Pearse Street, and then take the first right. It's number 2a / 2b / 2c on your map.

3 From Trinity College to St. Stephen's Green
Go back to Pearse Street and turn left, then left into College Street and then Grafton Street, and finally Nassau Street. Turn right into Dawson Street, and go straight ahead until the end. You can see it in front of you. It's number 3a / 3b / 3c on your map.

4 From St. Stephen's Green to the National Gallery
Come out of St. Stephen's Green and go down Kildare Street. At the end, turn right, and go straight on down Clare Street. The National Gallery is on your right, number 4a / 4b / 4c on your map.

LEARN TO check and correct directions

4A Look at the map and correct A's information in sentences 1–6.

1 A: So, the park's between the cinema and the pharmacy.
   B: No, it's _behind_ the cinema and the pharmacy.

2 A: So the supermarket's between the cinema and the pharmacy.
   B: No, it's between _____.

3 A: So, the cinema is the fourth building on the left.
   B: No, it's _____.

4 A: So, the café is the fourth building on the left.
   B: No, it's _____.

5 A: So, the post office is opposite the bank.
   B: No, it's opposite _____.

6 A: So, the town hall is opposite the bank.
   B: No, it's _____ the bank.

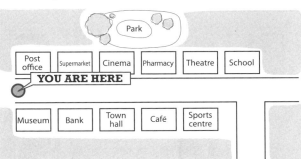

B Circle the stressed word in each of B's answers.

1 B: No, it's (behind) the cinema and the pharmacy.

C ▶ 7.3 Listen and check. Then listen and repeat.

GRAMMAR present continuous

1 Write the -ing form of the verbs.

1 do   _doing_
2 have   _____
3 run   _____
4 stay   _____
5 swim   _____
6 sleep   _____
7 write   _____
8 try   _____
9 begin   _____
10 give   _____

2A Complete the sentences with the present continuous form of the verbs.

1 Jake _'s playing_ (play) the guitar and _singing_ (sing).
2 Wesley _____ (take) a photo of Jake.
3 Jo and Sam _____ (stand) near Jake and _____ (listen) to him.
4 Roger _____ (walk) near Jake but he _____ (not listen) to him.
5 Megan _____ (sit) and _____ (drink) a coffee.
6 Paolo and Zoe _____ (chat) with each other. They _____ (not) watching Jake.
7 Lisa _____ (look) at some bags.
8 Philip _____ (sell) a bag to Kalila.

B Look at the picture and use the information in Exercise 2A to label the people.

C Write the questions.

1 What / Megan / read?
   What's Megan reading?
2 Who / Zoe / talk to?
   _____
3 Where / Zoe and Paolo / sit?
   _____
4 How many bags / Jo and Sam / carry?
   _____
5 Who / Wesley / take / a photo of?
   _____
6 What / Roger / do?
   _____
7 Who / laugh?
   _____
8 What / Zoe / drinking?
   _____

D Look at the picture below and answer the questions from Exercise 2C.

1 _She's reading a magazine._
2 _____
3 _____
4 _____
5 _____
6 _____
7 _____
8 _____

3 **Put the words in order to make questions. Then write short answers about you.**

1 you / are / shoes / wearing?
   Are you wearing shoes? Yes, I am. / No, I'm not.

2 your / is / ringing / phone?
   _____

3 are / pen / a / with / exercise / this / doing / you?
   _____

4 room / other / the / sitting / are / people / in / any?
   _____

5 music / is / room / the / in / playing?
   _____

6 exercise / enjoying / are / this / you?
   _____

7 teacher / is / your / writing / the / board /on?
   _____

8 your / drinking / classmates / coffee / are?
   _____

VOCABULARY verbs with prepositions

4 **Complete the sentences with prepositions.**

1 Kim's over there. He's chatting _to_____ Joan.
2 I'm waiting _____ the train.
3 Diana, can you take a photo _____ the class?
4 What are you listening _____?
5 We read _____ the wedding yesterday in the newspaper.
6 I can't come at the moment. I'm _____ the phone.
7 Hazel is on holiday. At the moment she's lying _____ a beach in Goa.
8 Harry looked _____ his watch. Jean was thirty minutes late.

LISTENING

5A ▶ 8.1 **Listen and match phone conversations 1–5 with the correct places a)–e).**

Conversation 1   a) tennis match
Conversation 2   b) fashion show
Conversation 3   c) art gallery
Conversation 4   d) concert
Conversation 5   e) ticket office

B **Listen again and underline the correct alternative for each conversation.**

1 The woman *really likes / doesn't like* the paintings.
2 Nellie *wants / doesn't want* to go to the concert.
3 The woman is *in / going into* a concert.
4 Felicity says she *wants / doesn't want* to meet for a coffee.
5 *All / Some of* the people are wearing black.

WRITING pronouns

6A **Read the story. Who took Julia's phone?**

On Friday night, David, Julia and I went to the Rock Club. [1]Julia and David are fun and I like [2]Julia and David a lot. The club was busy, but [3]David, Julia and I found a table.

Julia put her mobile phone on the table, but after an hour [4]Julia saw that [5]Julia's phone wasn't there, and she was very angry. Then I had a good idea. I phoned [6]Julia's number, and [7]Julia, David and I heard [8]Julia's phone ringing.

David started laughing, and then [9]David took Julia's phone out of [10]David's pocket and gave [11]Julia's phone back to [12]Julia. David thought this was funny, but Julia was very angry with [13]David, so she took [14]David's phone and threw [15]David's phone out of the window! Now [16]David and Julia aren't speaking to each other.

B **Replace the underlined nouns in the story with pronouns.**

1 _They_____
2 _____
3 _____
4 _____
5 _____
6 _____
7 _____
8 _____
9 _____
10 _____
11 _____
12 _____
13 _____
14 _____
15 _____
16 _____

VOCABULARY appearance

1A Read sentences 1–6 below and label the men in the picture.

1 William's got long dark hair. He's very slim.
2 Tom's got long dark hair and a moustache. He's slim.
3 Mike's got short dark hair and a moustache. He's slim.
4 Sam's got very short dark hair and a beard. He isn't very slim.
5 Robert's got short dark hair, a moustache and a beard. He's very slim.
6 Bruce's got short dark hair. He isn't very slim.

B Describe the women in the picture.

1 Meg*'s got long blonde hair and she's slim.*
2 Belinda _____
3 Jay _____
4 Keira _____

GRAMMAR present simple/continuous

2 Underline the correct alternatives.

Gerald: Hi, Bruno. It's me, Gerald. What ¹*do you do / are you doing?*

Bruno: I ²*have / 'm having* a coffee with Carla. What about you?

Gerald: I ³*sit / 'm sitting* at my desk as usual. So you ⁴*don't work / aren't working* today.

Bruno: I am, but I ⁵*don't usually start / 'm not usually starting* work before ten o'clock.

Gerald: How's Carla?

Bruno: OK, but she ⁶*doesn't like / isn't liking* her job at the hospital.

Gerald: Oh, why not?

Bruno: Well, she ⁷*works / 's working* from 11 a.m. till midnight every day.

Gerald: That sounds hard. ⁸*Does she look / Is she looking* for a new job?

Bruno: Yes, I think so. She ⁹*looks / is looking* in the newspaper and on the internet every day.

Gerald: Really? Because ¹⁰*I phone / I'm phoning* about a job opening here. Office work, not very interesting but the money isn't bad. Perfect for Carla.

Bruno: Hey, Carla – good news, it's Gerald ...

3 Complete the conversations with the present simple or present continuous form of the verbs in brackets.

Conversation 1

A: So who does the housework in your family?

B: We all ¹ *do* _____ (do) it. In fact my wife ²_____ (cook) dinner right now, and my daughter ³_____ (help) her.

A: And what ⁴_____ you _____ (do) to help at the moment?

B: I ⁵_____ (watch) TV! There are too many people in the kitchen.

Conversation 2

A: Why ⁶_____ (wear) black today? You ⁷_____ (not usually wear) black.

B: What do you mean? I always ⁸_____ (wear) it!

Conversation 3

A: Hi, Geoff. It's me. Where are you?

B: I ⁹_____ (stand) on the train.

A: Why? You ¹⁰_____ usually _____ (not stand).

B: No, I usually ¹¹_____ (get) a seat, but this is a later train. Where are you?

A: I ¹²_____ (wait) at the station.

B: Oh, sorry. I forgot to tell you I'm late!

VOCABULARY clothes

4 Use the pictures to complete the crossword.

Across:

Down:

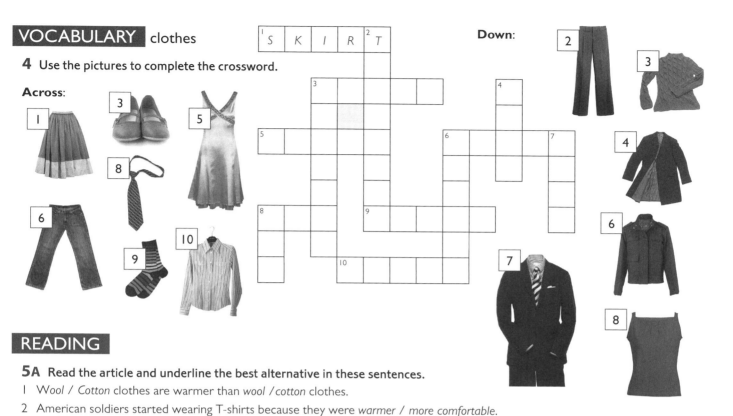

S K I R T

READING

5A Read the article and underline the best alternative in these sentences.

1 *Wool* / *Cotton* clothes are warmer than *wool* / *cotton* clothes.
2 American soldiers started wearing T-shirts because they were *warmer* / *more comfortable*.
3 Now people wear T-shirts because they're *comfortable and cheap* / *popular all over the world*.

THE T-SHIRT IS HERE TO STAY

It's hard to think of life without T-shirts. But the word 'T-shirt' only became a word in the English dictionary in the 1920s, and the style only became popular in the 1960s.

In the Second World War, American soldiers wore wool uniforms, and they were very hot and uncomfortable in the European summers. The American soldiers saw that European soldiers weren't hot because they wore a light cotton vest under their shirt. After that, all the soldiers in the American army started wearing cotton vests.

So men wore T-shirts <u>under</u> their shirts – T-shirts were underwear. Then in the 1950s, three American film stars (John Wayne, Marlon Brando and James Dean) surprised everyone by wearing their 'underwear' in films.

In the 1960s, it became easier to put words and pictures on T-shirts. By the late 60s, rock and roll bands and sports teams started to make big money selling T-shirts with their logos and team names on them.

After that, T-shirts became popular not just in the USA, but all over the world. People wear T-shirts to express themselves with words and slogans and because they are comfortable, cheap and can be fun. T-shirts will be popular for a long, long time.

B Are the sentences true (T) or false (F)?

1 T-shirts became popular in the 1920s.   *F*
2 American soldiers brought T-shirts to Europe.
3 For many years T-shirts were underwear.
4 American movie stars surprised people when they took their T-shirts off.
5 Putting pictures on T-shirts started in the 1980s.
6 T-shirts are popular all over the world.

C Match the words from the article with their definitions.

1 uniform
2 light
3 vest
4 logo
5 to express
6 slogan

a) a piece of underwear that people (often men) can wear under a shirt or top
b) special clothes that people wear for a job or school
c) to show your feelings, your ideas or your personality
d) a short, clever phrase that an organisation uses, e.g. Nike's 'Just do it.'
e) not heavy; good in hot weather
f) a symbol for a group or an organisation, e.g. the Apple Computer Company's apple.

VOCABULARY types of film

1A Add the vowels.

1 act_i_ _o_ n f_i_lm
2 h__rr__r f__lm
3 sc__-f__ f__lm
4 m__s__c__l
5 r__m__nt__c f__lm
6 c__m__dy
7 dr__m__

B Match the film reviews with the types of film above.

A

Ninety minutes in the scary world of vampires and blood ... 2

B

Childhood friends Jessica and Tim meet after ten years, and they want to be more than just good friends ...

C

Gene Walker is a modern-day Fred Astaire, dancing and singing his way through the streets of Cordoba ...

D

New York police officer Jack Hare takes a holiday in Miami, but finds himself working to save the country from a terrorist attack ...

E

A farmer in France wakes up and finds that all his animals can speak ... Chinese. Lots of laughs as the farmer teaches himself Chinese to talk to the animals.

F

A small Indian village has a visit from space tourists – aliens from another galaxy. A surprise as the aliens have more to learn from the locals than they think ...

G

Sally Bonner loses her parents in a train accident. She is blind and grows up alone with no friends ... but then Edmund, her teacher, helps Sally learn to play the piano.

FUNCTION recommending

2 Put the words in the box in the correct places in the conversation. You do not need two of the words.

| ~~recommend~~ about borrow I name in called you kind |

A: Do you want to watch a film?

B: Sorry, I'm busy.

A: Oh. Well then, ¹can you *recommend* a good film?

B: Hmmm ... ²What of films do you like?

A: Horror films, action films ...

B: Do you like sci-fi?

A: I don't know many sci-fi films.

B: ³There's a good film *The Matrix*.

A: ⁴What's it?

B: It's about the future and the way machines control us ...

A: ⁵Who's it?

B: Keanu Reeves, Laurence Fishburne ... Carrie-Ann Moss.

A: Oh, she's good. ⁶Do you think 'd like it?

B: Yeah, I think so. It's very exciting. I really enjoyed it.

A: ⁷Can I it?

B: Oh, I haven't got it, but you can rent it from the DVD shop.

A: OK, thanks.

LEARN TO link words

3A 8.2 Listen and write the consonant-vowel links in the sentences below.

1 Are you looking for_a film?
2 Is it an action film?
3 Is anyone famous in it?
4 Do you want to borrow a DVD?
5 I haven't got a DVD player.
6 I've got it on video.

B Listen again and repeat.

C 8.3 Listen and circle the sentence you hear.

1 a) Are you looking for a film?
  b) Are you looking for a friend?
2 a) Is it an action film?
  b) Is it an interesting film?
3 a) Is Anna Faris in it?
  b) Is anyone famous in it?
4 a) Do you want to borrow a DVD?
  b) Do you want to buy a DVD?
5 a) I haven't got a DVD player.
  b) I haven't got a CD player.
6 a) I've got it on video.
  b) I've got an old video.

VOCABULARY transport collocations

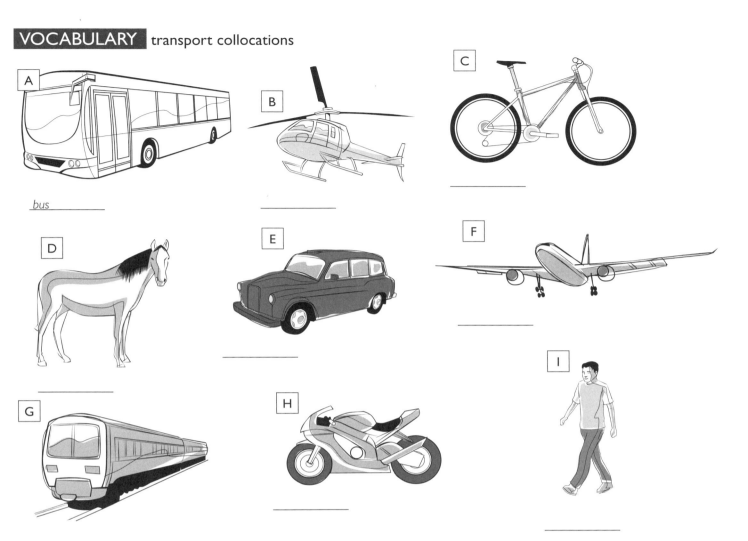

A — bus

B — _____

C — _____

D — _____

E — _____

F — _____

G — _____

H — _____

I — _____

1A Label pictures A–I.

B Match sentences 1–9 with pictures A–I.

1 It's got two wheels, you get on and off it and it doesn't use petrol.   C

2 It's usually got two pilots and can carry a lot of people.

3 It's got four wheels and you pay the driver at the end of the journey.

4 It's got four legs and you ride it.

5 It's got two wheels and it uses petrol.

6 It's got a lot of wheels and you need a ticket.

7 It hasn't got any wheels and it can't carry a lot of people.

8 It hasn't got any wheels, it uses no petrol, and it's free.

9 It's got four or more wheels and you pay at the start of the journey.

2 Complete the conversations with the correct form of the verbs below.

| get off   go by (×2)   go on   take   ride   come by   get on |

1 **A:** Can you tell me the way to the Sports Centre?

   B: Yes, you take the number 195 bus and you _get off_ at the third stop.

2 **A:** How did you travel to Paris?

   B: I _____ train.

3 **A:** Is this Kenji's first bike?

   B: Yes, and he _____ it everywhere.

4 **A:** What's the best way to get to the airport?

   B: You can go by bus or you can _____ a taxi.

5 **A:** How do you go to school?

   B: I usually _____ foot.

6 **A:** How does Stefanie go to work?

   B: She _____ car.

7 **A:** Where are you?

   B: I'm at Berlin airport and I _____ a plane to South Africa, so I can't talk.

8 **A:** Did you drive here?

   B: No, I _____ bus.

READING

3A Read the article and circle the correct answers.

1 A *commute* is …
   a) a type of transport
   b) the journey from home to work and back
   c) a part of a car.

2 Jim Kendrick won $10,000 because …
   a) he was the safest driver in Texas
   b) he drove the most kilometres in one year
   c) he travelled the furthest to work.

DO YOU THINK YOUR COMMUTE IS BAD? TRY 640 KILOMETRES A DAY!

Do you think gas* prices are too high? Well, be happy that you aren't Jim Kendrick of Texas in the USA.

5 Every weekday, Kendrick drives 320 kilometres from his home in San Antonio, Texas, to his job at AbleCargo in the port of Houston … and then 320
10 kilometres back again! He leaves work at 5a.m. and gets home and has dinner with his wife at 9p.m.

For his daily journey, Kendrick
15 won the competition 'America's Longest Commute'. His three-and-a-half-hour commute was longer than all the other people in the competition, and
20 is a lot more than the average American commute of twenty-five minutes.

'I was surprised to win,' said Kendrick, who won $10,000.
25 'I was sure that someone else had a longer commute. But it's great – $10,000 is just enough to buy gas for another year.'

Why does he do it? 'Well, my
30 wife and I have a beautiful house in San Antonio and our lifestyle is important to us.'

'The drive gives me a lot of energy. Sometimes, when I
35 drive my Ford Mustang down the highway, I feel like a professional racing car driver.'

How much longer does he want to do this commute? 'Another
40 five or ten years,' Kendrick said. 'I don't see any reason to stop. But gas prices are high, so maybe I need to look for a job nearer home.'

*gas (American English) = petrol (British English)

B Match sentence halves 1–6 with a)–f). Write the line number from the article where you found the information.

1 Jim won the contest because _f – line 16_
2 He was surprised to win because _____
3 He was happy about the money because _____
4 He does the commute because _____
5 He feels good when he drives because _____
6 He's thinking about changing jobs because _____

a) he doesn't want to change his lifestyle.
b) he spends about $10,000 a year on gas.
c) he thought someone else drove further.
d) gas prices are so high.
e) he feels like a racing car driver.
f) his commute was the longest.

GRAMMAR articles

4 Complete the text with *a/an*, *the* or no article (-).

Jim lives in [1] _a_ house near [2] _____ San Antonio, Texas. He's got [3] _____ job at AbleCargo in [4] _____ Houston, Texas, in [5] _____ USA. AbleCargo is [6] _____ shipping company, and Jim's [7] _____ engineer there. He drives seven hours every day, and gets [8] _____ home at 8.30 and has [9] _____ dinner at 9p.m. He likes [10] _____ fast cars, and he drives [11] _____ Ford Mustang. Jim doesn't commute at [12] _____ weekend.

5 Add *the* (×6) and *a/an* (×4) to these sentences. One sentence does not need any extra words.

1 Yes, *the* bus station is down this street on left.
2 Rajiv is actor in Mumbai.
3 I haven't got car, but I've got motorbike.
4 Town Hall opens at 9.30 in morning.
5 I love planes and flying. I always ask for window seat.
6 Keith often works at home in evening.
7 Is Manchester in UK?
8 I often go home by taxi at night.

VOCABULARY adjectives (1)

1A Complete the adjectives in this article about transport.

HOW DO YOU TRAVEL AROUND THE CITY?

I go to work by rollerblades. It's a ¹fast_____ way to travel and it's very ²hea_____ because I get lots of exercise.

Sometimes it feels quite ³dan_____ with so many cars around me, and it's a little ⁴inc_____ because I need to change into shoes when I go into my office. But roller blades are a lot of fun.

Tony Jones, film producer

rollerblades

I go everywhere by skateboard. True, it takes a long time to learn because it's ⁵dif_____ to ride one, but it's very ⁶con_____ – when I go into a shop I just pick up the skateboard and carry it like a book!

Joel Williams, musician

skateboard

I use my scooter all around the city. It's ⁷saf_____, it's ⁸eas_____ to ride and it's more ⁹com_____ than roller blades or a skateboard, because balancing isn't a problem. Sometimes you see scooters with motors on them, but those are really ¹⁰pol_____. 'Go green,' I say!

Nanci Levine, student

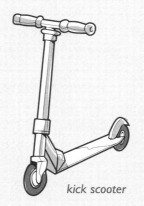

kick scooter

B ▶ 9.1 Listen and check.

C Listen again and repeat. Write the adjectives in the correct place according to the stress.

1 O	2 Oo
fast	
3 Ooo	4 oOo
5 oOoo	6 ooOoo

READING

2A Read the article. How does the writer feel?

happy relaxed angry hungry funny

No more wheels!
A shopkeeper speaks out

'I have a small food shop in the city centre, and I really don't like customers coming into the shop on wheels. A businessman comes in on a kick scooter, and he thinks it's funny to do his shopping on the scooter. I don't think it's funny, I think it's dangerous. And the skateboarders, they're even worse. They say they ride skateboards because it's fast and convenient, you know, it's easy to pick up the skateboard when they walk into a shop, but they don't pick up the skateboard, they ride it up and down my shop. But the worst of all are the rollerbladers. They fly into the shop, of course they don't take off the rollerblades because it's inconvenient, and they crash into customers and knock things down. It's terrible! So now I have a new rule: No more wheels. Shoes only!'

B Read the article again. Are sentences 1–6 true (T) or false (F)?

1 The writer has a restaurant. *F*
2 He thinks the businessman is a funny person.
3 To the writer, kick scooters are not safe.
4 He thinks kick scooters are are better than skateboards.
5 Skateboarders usually pick up their skateboards when they're in his shop.
6 Rollerbladers are the most dangerous, he thinks.

GRAMMAR *can/can't, have to/don't have to*

3A Complete the conversations with the correct form of *can*.

1 A: *Can I park* _____ my car here? (I / park)

B: No, _____. (you / not)

2 A: _____ your bike on the pavement because it's too dangerous. (You / not / ride)

B: Oh, OK.

3 A: _____ on the train? (people / smoke)

B: No, _____. (they / not)

4 A: _____ to the theatre? (we / walk)

B: Yes, _____, but it's a long way. (we)

5 A: _____ into the city centre, but not cars. (Taxis / drive)

B: OK, thanks.

B Complete the conversations with *can't* or *don't have to.*

Conversation 1

A: What clothes do you have to wear for the new job?

B: I *don't have to* ____ wear a suit and tie, but I have to wear a white shirt and I _____ wear jeans.

Conversation 2

A: It's late ... after midnight.

B: Yes, but we _____ get up early tomorrow. It's Saturday.

Conversation 3

A: You _____ drive down this road. It's for buses only.

B: Oh, sorry.

Conversation 4

A: I haven't got any money with me.

B: It's OK. You _____ pay me now. Give me the money tomorrow.

4 Underline the correct alternatives.

A: Hey, do you want to do something tonight? I [1]*can't / don't have to* work.

B: Let's see ... No, I [2]*can't / don't have to* meet you tonight – I [3]*can / have to* work late.

A: Well, [4]*can we / do we have to* meet tomorrow?

B: Sorry, I [5]*can't / don't have to*, I'm busy. But I [6]*can / have to* do something on Saturday.

A: Great. We [7]*can / have to* go to that new Italian restaurant, La Spezia.

B: Hmm ... Saturday night is usually crowded. [8]*Can we / Do we have to* book a table or [9]*can we / do we have to* just go there?

A: It isn't so popular now, so we [10]*can't / don't have to* book. And if we [11]*can't / don't have to* get a table, we [12]*can / have to* go somewhere else.

B: Great! See you on Saturday, then.

LISTENING

5A Look at the picture of Carin Van Buren on her balancing scooter. Do you think the statements are true (T) or false (F)?

1 It's difficult to ride.

2 You can ride it on the pavement.

3 In a city it's faster than a bus.

4 It's tiring to ride.

B ▶ 9.2 Listen and check.

C Listen again and answer the questions.

1 Does Carin ride the scooter to work?
Yes, she does. _____

2 How did she travel to work before?
_____

3 How long does it take to learn?
_____

4 How fast can the scooter go?
_____

5 Does she think a scooter is better than a bike?
_____

6 Where does she leave her scooter at work?
_____

7 How does she feel when people laugh at her on her scooter?
_____

8 Does she like it when people stop her and ask her questions?
_____

VOCABULARY excuses

1 Complete the excuses.

1 I didn't h_e_ _a_ _r_ my al _ _ _ _ cl _ _ _ _.
2 We slept late and mi _ _ _ _ our plane.
3 I lo _ _ my ke _ _.
4 My car br _ _ _ _ d _ _ _ _.
5 The traf _ _ _ was b _ _.

FUNCTION apologising

2A Put the words in the correct order to complete the conversation.

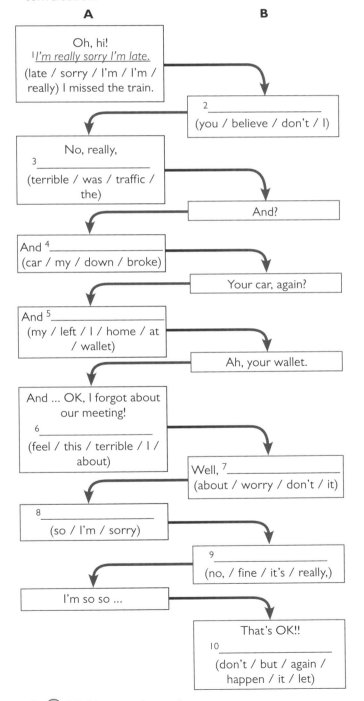

A

Oh, hi!
1 *I'm really sorry I'm late.*
(late / sorry / I'm / I'm / really) I missed the train.

B

2 _____
(you / believe / don't / I)

No, really,
3 _____
(terrible / was / traffic / the)

And?

And 4_____
(car / my / down / broke)

Your car, again?

And 5_____
(my / left / I / home / at / wallet)

Ah, your wallet.

And ... OK, I forgot about our meeting!
6 _____
(feel / this / terrible / I / about)

Well, 7_____
(about / worry / don't / it)

8 _____
(so / I'm / sorry)

9 _____
(no, / fine / it's / really,)

I'm so so ...

That's OK!!
10 _____
(don't / but / again / happen / it / let)

B ▶ 9.3 Listen and repeat.

LEARN TO tell a long story

3 Write Bruce's email from the notes.

Dear Alexis,
I'm really sorry about last night. I know it was your birthday. But I had an unlucky evening ...
First of all, I / leave / the house late because I / lose / my keys.
Then I / miss / the bus, so I / phone / a taxi, but the taxi / break down / and I / wait / thirty minutes for another taxi.
After that, I / get / to the restaurant an hour late, but I / leave / your present in the taxi.
I / phone / the taxi company, but they / not answer, so I / go / into the restaurant, but you / not be there.
Finally, I / go / home and / try / to phone you, but you / not answer.
Now I don't know what to do. I'm really sorry.
Love,
Bruce

First of all, I left the house late because ... _____

_____
_____
_____
_____
_____
_____
_____
_____
_____
_____

VOCABULARY airport

4 Put the letters of the words in brackets in the correct order to complete the story.

We had a terrible time at the airport. We missed our train and arrived forty minutes before the plane 1 *took off* _____ (okto fof). We ran to the desk,2_____ (deckche ni) and got our boarding passes. Then we went through 3_____ (irucytes) and 4_____ (protsaps nolcrot) – no problems. In the 5_____ (pratedeur gunole) we didn't do any 6_____ (xat-refe pishpong) because we only had ten minutes. We ran to the 7_____ (teag), but we were too late so we didn't 8_____ (teg no) the plane. What a disaster!

GRAMMAR verb forms

1A Underline the correct alternatives.

jesse's festival blog

Jesse McCormack is a member of the rock group the Stringers. He ¹*writes* / *is writing* most of the band's songs and ²*plays* / *is playing* lead guitar. This is his summer festival blog.

Saturday 4th August

I ³*write* / *'m writing* my blog today at our fourth festival this summer ... but it's the biggest with more than 25,000 people and we ⁴*have* / *'re having* a great time. The atmosphere here is amazing and people are very friendly. We usually ⁵*arrive* / *are arriving* the day before we play, but this time we ⁶*come* / *came* here two days ago.

Most people have tents, but in fact you ⁷*don't have to* / *can't* sleep in a tent. You ⁸*can* / *can't* sleep in your car. And there are the usual festival rules, for example you ⁹*can* / *can't* use glasses for drinks – you ¹⁰*have to* / *don't have to* use plastic cups. This is a good idea because sometimes people, often children, ¹¹*walk* / *are walking* around with no shoes on.

There's only one hour before we start our show. Danny ¹²*talks* / *'s talking* to a woman from Radio One. Saul ¹³*practises* / *is practising* our first song. Our manager, Dave, ¹⁴*calls* / *is calling* us so I ¹⁵*have to* / *can* stop now. More tomorrow!

B Complete the interview with the correct form of the present simple or present continuous.

Janna: This is Janna Towli from Radio One and I ¹*'m talking*_____ (talk) to Danny Wright from the Stringers. Hi, Danny.

Danny: Hi, everyone.

Janna: So Danny, ²_____ (you / enjoy) yourself at the festival?

Danny: Yeah, it's cool.

Janna: We've got some questions. First, from Luka. He asks: ³'_____ (Jesse / write) all the songs or ⁴_____ (you / write) any of them?'

Danny: Oh, Jesse is the songwriter. I just ⁵_____ (sing) the songs.

Janna: And from Viktoria: 'What's your favourite Stringers song?'

Danny: Erm ... *You never* ⁶_____ (say) '*I love you.*'

Janna: OK, right. And the last question, from Abby. She asks: 'What ⁷_____ (Danny / wear) today?'

Danny: Me? Well, today I ⁸_____ (wear) a Stringers T-shirt and jeans. My usual! Oh, there's Dave, our manager. I have to go.

Janna: Thanks for talking to us. Good luck with the show!

Danny: Thanks!

VOCABULARY alphabet puzzle

2 Complete the sentences with words beginning with the letters A–Z.

A I'm sorry I'm late. I didn't hear my _**alarm**_ clock.

B My grandfather had a moustache and a big black _**beard**_ .

C The tram stop is close to my flat, so it's very _____ for me.

D Riding a bike is quite _____, so you have to wear a helmet.

E The opposite of a *crowded* beach is an _____ beach.

F The White House is one of the most _____ buildings in the world.

G I want to see the Eiffel Tower. Where do I _____ off the bus?

H *Frankenstein* was one of the first _____ films. It was quite scary.

I The opposite of *boring* is _____.

J The Amazon _____ is 7 million square kilometres.

K Do you _____ the way to the bus station?

L François is _____ on his bed. He doesn't feel very well.

M I got up late and I _____ my train.

N The children in the next room are too _____ – I can't work.

O Do you go by car or _____ foot?

P Cars are more _____ than bikes. Bikes are greener.

Q Be _____! The baby's sleeping.

R Can you _____ a good DVD?

S Tourists always visit Red _____ in Moscow.

T I was late because the _____ was bad.

U Alan's shoes are too small, so they're very _____.

V She was born in a small _____ in Belgium.

W The traffic is _____ at five o'clock than at three o'clock.

X How do you spell the opposite of *cheap*? e_____

Y Hi, Liz. It's Jon. I waited for _____ for two hours! What happened?

Z My holiday was great. We saw the Great Wall. It was ama_____!

comparatives and superlatives

3 Complete the information with the correct comparative or superlative form of the words in the box.

| tall | cheap | hot | quiet | interesting | ~~good~~ | slow | convenient | cold | fast |

SHANGHAI

When is the best time to go?

The ¹ _best_ months to visit are May and October, when it's 19–24°C. July and August are ² _____ months, when it can be 28°C. November to April are ³ _____ months, when it's 3–14°C.

How can I get around?

You can travel by bus or by metro. Buses are ⁴ _____ than the metro, especially in the morning and evening when the traffic is bad. The metro is ⁵ _____ than buses, but there are only two metro lines. The ⁶ _____ way to travel around the city is by taxi because there are lots – they go everywhere and they aren't very expensive.

I only have one day! What can I see?

Visit ⁷ _____ building in China, the 492-metre Shanghai World Financial Centre. The floor is glass and it feels like walking in the sky. Walk along the Bund, next to the river – it's very central, but it's a lot ⁸ _____ than the noisy city centre. And visit the Shanghai Museum – most visitors to the city say this is ⁹ _____ thing to see in Shanghai.

Where can I stay?

Shanghai has hundreds of hotels, and there are many two-star and three-star hotels for travellers on a budget – of course, these are ¹⁰ _____ than the 4-star luxury hotels. Check the internet for recommendations from other travellers.

FUNCTION recommending; giving directions

4A ▶ RC 3.1 Listen to the conversations and choose the correct ending to the sentence.

Jurgen recommends a restaurant to Greg but ...

a) Greg doesn't understand and takes the wrong street.

b) he gives bad directions and Greg and doesn't find the restaurant.

c) Greg decides to stay home and eat pizza.

B Listen again. Are the sentences true (T) or false (F)?

1 It's Jurgen's wife's birthday.   _F_

2 Greg and his wife like Chinese food.

3 Jurgen recommends a Chinese restaurant.

4 The restaurant is near the pharmacy.

5 Greg and his wife find the restaurant.

6 They have pizza at the restaurant.

C Listen again and complete the sentences.

1 What kind of food _do you like_ ?

2 Do you think my wife _____?

3 Can you tell _____?

4 Go down Hillside Road past the pharmacy _____.

5 Then go straight _____ 200 metres.

6 Oh, no – I'm so _____.

7 I feel terrible _____.

8 Don't worry _____.

GRAMMAR articles

5 Complete the text with a/an, the or no article (-).

POLAND – DAY 7

The best way to see ¹ _the_ city of ² _____ Krakow is in ³ _____ Trabant – the classic eastern-European car. The tour starts at 9.00a.m. in ⁴ _____ city centre, where you meet your tour guides Irek and Kasia. Irek is ⁵ _____ university student and Kasia is ⁶ _____ history teacher, and together they know Krakow better than most professional guides. You start the tour on ⁷ _____ foot and visit Cloth Hall in ⁸ _____ centre of Grand Square. You then go by ⁹ _____ car and visit Nowa Huta and the Jewish quarter. Lunch is at ¹⁰ _____ restaurant near the castle. ¹¹ _____ Polish food is quite rich, so try not to eat too much! In ¹² _____ afternoon, Irek and Kasia can show you Wawel Castle or take you back to your hotel.

TEST

Circle the correct option to complete the sentences.

1   Sitting on the beach is _____ working.
   a) relaxing than   b) better than   c) more nice than

2   There was a bridge over the _____.
   a) desert   b) river   c) mountain

3   I _____ my MP3 player.
   a) listening to   b) 'm listenning to   c) 'm listening to

4   What _____ like?
   a) does Jon look   b) Jon does look   c) Jon looks

5   A: Do I _____ the bus here for the museum?
   B: No, at the next stop.
   a) go by   b) ride   c) get off

6   I didn't get a seat because the train was _____.
   a) comfortable   b) uncomfortable   c) crowded

7   Sorry I'm late. I _____ my train.
   a) lost   b) missed   c) left

8   A: What _____?
   B: I'm working on the computer.
   a) you are doing   b) are you doing   c) do you doing?

9   I don't think _____ this DVD. It's too scary.
   a) you'd like   b) you like
   c) you recommend

10   My wife works _____. She's a writer.
   a) at home   b) at the home   c) home

11   _____ to the airport by bus?
   a) You can go   b) Do you can go   c) Can you go

12   Go _____ until the end of the street.
   a) straight   b) straight on   c) strait on

13   It was difficult to walk in the _____ because of all the trees.
   a) mountain   b) jungle   c) village

14   The children _____ very well at the moment.
   a) aren't feeling   b) don't feeling   c) aren't feel

15   He _____ slim with short black hair.
   a) 's got   b) 's   c) has

16   Spanish is _____ than English.
   a) easyer   b) easier   c) more easy

17   Children _____ pay. It's free for them.
   a) don't have to   b) can't   c) haven't to

18   A: I laughed a lot at this DVD. It's very funny.
   B: Oh, so it's a _____.
   a) drama   b) musical   c) comedy

19   A: Is there a post office near here?
   B: Yes, go down here and it's _____.
   a) on the left   b) on left   c) left

20   I always go by underground because it's fast and _____ .
   a) convenient   b) polluting   c) dangerous

21   It's _____ hotel in Saudi Arabia.
   a) the bigger   b) the bigest   c) the biggest

22   The sign says 'No Smoking' so you _____ smoke here.
   a) have to   b) don't have to   c) can't

23   My grandmother is _____.
   a) in sixties   b) in her sixties   c) in the sixties

24   A: Do you often phone your parents?
   B: Yes, I talked to _____ last night.
   a) them   b) him and her   c) they

25   _____ are good for you.
   a) Vegetables   b) The vegetables   c) Vegetable

26   Who is _____ player in the football team?
   a) most bad   b) the worst   c) the baddest

27   _____, the train arrived. It was four hours late.
   a) First of all   b) After   c) Finally

28   Leonie _____ black.
   a) always is wearing
   b) is wearing always   c) always wears

29   A: Where's the tourist information centre?
   B: You _____ left and walk for about five minutes.
   a) take   b) turn to   c) turn

30   A: Have you got _____?
   B: No, I haven't, but I've got two brothers.
   a) a sister   b) the sister   c) sister

TEST RESULT | **/30**

GRAMMAR *be going to; would like to*

1A Look at the table and complete sentences 1–10 with the correct form of *be going to* or *would like to*.

	Plans next week	Plans next year	Wishes for the future
Jim, USA	start new job at the bank – Monday	look for a new flat / not stay at parents' house	be very rich
Soo Min, South Korea	have haircut – Tuesday	go to university	work in TV
Bill and Jane, Ireland	visit daughter Lynn and family – Sat/Sun	not have a holiday	move nearer Lynn

1 Jim *'s going to start* _____ his new job at the bank on Monday.
2 He _____ for a new flat next year.
3 He _____ at his parents' house.
4 He _____ very rich.
5 Soo Min _____ a haircut on Tuesday.
6 She _____ to university next year.
7 She _____ in TV.
8 Bill and Jane _____ their daughter at the weekend.
9 They _____ a holiday next year.
10 They _____ nearer their daughter.

B Write questions for the people with *be going to* or *would like to.*

1 Which bank / you / work at, Jim?
   Which bank are you going to work at, Jim?
2 Where / you / look for / a new flat, Jim?

3 When / you / go / to university, Soo Min?

4 Why / like / work / in TV, Soo Min?

5 How / you / travel, Bill and Jane?

6 Why / like / move / nearer your daughter, Bill and Jane?

C Match answers a)–f) with questions 1–6 in Exercise 1B.
a) Because I want to be famous.   4
b) We're going by train.
c) In the city centre.
d) We'd like to see our grandchildren more.
e) In September next year.
f) At HSBC bank.

2 Put the words in order to make questions. Then write short answers about you.
1 TV / you / to / evening / watch / are / this / going?
   Are you going to watch TV this evening?
   Yes, I am. / No, I'm not.
2 like / work / would / TV / to / you / in?

3 weekend / you / family / see / next / are / to / going / your?

4 for / English / to / useful / be / you / is / going?

5 like / new / would / phone / a / you / buy / to / mobile?

6 your / study / classmates / year / you / going / English / next / to / are / and?

7 in / like / live / country / you / to / would / another?

8 home / your / like / now / to / go / would / classmates?

READING

3A Read the article and circle the best title.

1 Lottery winners around the world

2 Sisters win lottery

3 Another teenage lottery winner

First there was Tracey Makin in 1998, then Michael Carroll in 2002, and then Callie Rogers in 2003 – all of them were teenagers when they won the lottery. Tracey was sixteen at the time and won £1,055,171. Callie was the same age when she won £1,800,000 and Michael was nineteen when he won £9,700,000.

Now eighteen-year-old Ianthe Fullagar is the newest in this group of teenage lottery winners. She won £7,000,000 and we asked her about her future.

'I'm not going to change my plans very much. I'm still going to go to university. I'm going to live like a normal student and not a millionaire. I love my baked beans on toast.'

It was only the second time that she played the EuroMillions Lottery. She bought her ticket from a newsagent's and watched the lottery result on television.

First on her shopping list is a holiday in Egypt and a replacement for her ten-year-old Ford Ka. 'I'm going to fly to Cairo and spend about a month travelling around the country. When I come back, I'm going to sell my old car and buy a new one. I'd like to get a bigger one.'

B Read the article again and answer the questions.

1 Who won the largest amount of money?
Michael Carroll

2 Who won the smallest amount of money?
_____

3 Who are the youngest teenage winners?
_____

4 Does Ianthe want to change her life?
_____

5 Does she often buy lottery tickets?
_____

6 What is she going to do with the money?
_____

7 Why does she want to buy a new car?
_____

VOCABULARY plans

4A Complete the puzzle with the words from the box and find the message.

| ~~nothing~~ stay at buy clubbing learn a holiday start move a new suit go for |

```
            I
¹d  o  n  o  t  h  i  n  g
        2                   a  w  a  l  k
    ³g  e  t
            's
        ⁴h  a  v  e
        ⁵g  o
            6           h  o  u  s  e
7                   a  h  o  t  e  l
    8               a  n  e  w  j  o  b
            e
    9           t  o  s  w  i  m
    10          a  b  o  a  t
```

Message: _____ .

B Complete the conversations.

Conversation 1

A: What are you going to do this weekend?

B: I'm going jogging_____ on Saturday morning and then in the evening I'm going to meet Bob and we're going for a dr_____ in the pub.

Conversation 2

A: So, what are your plans?

B: Well, we're going to get ma_____ next year and we'd like to mo_____ to another country, maybe Spain. We'd like to bu_____ a house there, and start a fa_____, maybe have three or four children.

Conversation 3

A: What's your son going to do?

B: He's going to stay with some fr_____ in São Paulo. He wants to do a co_____ and le_____ Portuguese and then he'd like to get a jo_____ with a computer company in Brazil.

Conversation 4

A: What are you going to do with your lottery money?

B: First, I'm going to st_____ work! I'm going to ha_____ a big party, too. Then I want to bu_____ a big boat and tr_____ round the world!

Conversation 5

A: Are you going to buy pr_____ for all your friends?

B: Of course! And then I'm going to go sh_____ in Paris to buy some fantastic designer clothes.

VOCABULARY Phrases with *get*

1A Add the vowels to the adjectives.

1 Marco got _sunburnt_ (snbnt), so he ...
2 I got _____ (thrsty), so I ...
3 Adrian got _____ (brd) at school, so he ...
4 They got _____ (wt), so they...
5 Ed and Leo got _____ (hngry), so they ...
6 I got very _____ (ht), so I ...
7 Helena got _____ (lst), so she ...
8 We got _____ (cld), so we ...

B Match sentence halves 1–8 above with a)–h).

a) was an hour late for the meeting. 7
b) put on our coats.
c) had a second breakfast.
d) texted some of the other students in the class.
e) changed into dry clothes.
f) took off my sweater.
g) went for a drink with Carson.
h) stayed indoors for the next two days.

C ▶10.1 Listen and write the adjectives in the correct place according to the vowel sound.

1 /ʌ/ e.g. cup	2 /ɒ/ e.g. job	3 /e/ e.g. red
sunburnt		
4 /ɜː/ e.g. her	**5 /ɔː/ e.g. four**	**6 /əʊ/ e.g. go**

2 Look at the table and the meanings 1–4 of *get*. Write the words and phrases below in the correct column.

1 become	2 arrive	3 buy	4 obtain
get ...	get ...	get ...	get ...
hungry			

a hamburger   a new computer
  to school   lost
~~hungry~~   some help
  to work a new car
                home
a glass of water   a job   tired

LISTENING

3A ▶10.2 Listen to four people who survived in difficult situations. Match speakers 1–4 with places a)–d).

Speaker 1   a) jungle
Speaker 2   b) mountain
Speaker 3   c) desert
Speaker 4   d) sea

B Listen again and circle the best answers.

1 Speaker 1 _____.
  a) ate fish
  b) drank seawater
  c) was cold

2 Speaker 1 _____.
  a) got sunburnt
  b) got tired
  b) saw a lot of sharks

3 Speaker 2 _____.
  a) got cold
  b) walked all day
  c) got very thirsty

4 Speaker 2 _____.
  a) saw lots of insects
  b) had food with her
  c) sometimes took her shoes off

5 Speaker 3 _____.
  a) was on the mountain for three nights
  b) got lost because of the snow
  c) made a fire

6 Speaker 3 _____.
  a) slept on the ground
  b) got hungry
  c) stayed warm

7 Speaker 4 _____.
  a) got very hungry
  b) got thirsty
  c) didn't get bored

8 Speaker 4 _____.
  a) had some food with her
  b) ate plants
  c) ate insects

GRAMMAR *will, might, won't for prediction*

4 Complete sentences 1–8 with *'ll, will* or *won't* and a verb from the box.

~~get~~ be (×2) miss win come know love

1 Wear your coat or you<u>'ll get</u> cold.
2 Do you think Brazil _____ the World Cup?
3 It's very late. I'm sure the shop _____ open.
4 I don't want to go to the party! I _____ any people there.
5 Come on! We _____ the train.
6 Read this book. I'm sure you _____ it.
7 Oh no! I'm late again. The boss _____ happy.
8 You can invite Alain, but he _____. He doesn't like jazz music.

5 Underline the correct alternatives in the text.

SURVIVE IN THE CITY

People always talk about survival in the jungle, at sea, etc., but I'll tell you a really dangerous place: the city! Here are my tips for survival.

- Don't drive. Traffic is usually terrible and you ¹*might not / 'll / won't* spend more time in your car than seeing the city .

- Ask people for help – most people ²*will / might / won't* be happy to stop and help you.

- Don't stand in the street with a map in your hand and a camera around your neck. People ³*will / might not / won't* know you're a tourist. That's not a problem, but someone ⁴*will / might / might not* come and take your money.

- Wear normal clothes, not expensive ones. With expensive clothes, people ⁵*will / might not / won't* think you've got lots of money and yes – they ⁶*'ll / might / won't* take it away from you!

- Carry an umbrella. It often rains and with an umbrella you ⁷*'ll / might / won't* get wet.

- Don't stay out too late or it ⁸*'ll / might / might not* be easy to find a bus or a taxi.

- Give waiters a good tip, maybe 10%. You ⁹*'ll / might / might not* go back to the same restaurant and the waiter ¹⁰*will / might not / won't* forget you!

6 ▶ 10.3 Listen and number the sentences in the order you hear them.

1 a) You'll get cold.   2
  b) You get cold.   1
2 a) We'll miss the train.
  b) We miss the train.
3 a) I'm sure you'll hate it.
  b) I'm sure you hate it.
4 a) They'll know you're a tourist.
  b) They know you're a tourist.
5 a) I'll stay at home.
  b) I stay at home.
6 a) I'll never go out.
  b) I never go out.

WRITING *too, also, as well*

7 Are *too, also* and *as well* in the correct place? Tick three correct sentences. Correct the wrong sentences.

1 The bus is a good way to travel, and the underground is ⟨too⟩good.
2 If you buy a travel card for the underground, you can also use it on the bus.
3 You can ask shopkeepers for help – they're very friendly, and they'll know the city as well.
4 It's generally a safe city, but it can be dangerous also to walk alone late at night in some areas.
5 It isn't a good idea to carry a lot of money, and leave your expensive watch too at home.
6 You can get delicious food in cafés and as well in street markets.
7 Don't walk too far, and also wear comfortable shoes – then you won't get tired.
8 At night, taxis are as well convenient, but they're expensive.

8 Write a short text giving advice for a visitor to your town or city. Use *too, also, as well* and the phrases below to help you. Write 80–100 words.

The _____ is a good way to travel …
It's a good idea to carry …
You can ask _____ for help, and you can ask …
It can be dangerous to …

VOCABULARY adjectives

1 Put the letters in order to make adjectives. Start with the underlined letter.

1 zi<u>a</u>m<u>a</u>ng   _amazing_
2 cl<u>e</u>enextl   _____
3 o<u>c</u>lo   _____
4 relo<u>w</u>fund   _____
5 <u>f</u>nittfasac   _____
6 tare<u>g</u>   _____
7 owem<u>e</u>as   _____
8 tri<u>b</u>lilan   _____

FUNCTION making suggestions

2A Complete the conversation with the words in the box.

~~would~~ How don't about idea feel let's Why Have Sounds stay Brilliant

Tim: So, Gordon, what ¹ _would_ you like do today?
Gordon: I don't know. ² _____ you got any ideas?
Tim: What ³ _____ going to a concert?
Gordon: Hmmm ... That might be difficult. We ⁴ _____ like the same music. You like rock, I like hip-hop.
Tim: Oh. That's true. ⁵ _____ about inviting some friends?
Gordon: I don't really ⁶ _____ like doing that.
Tim: OK then. ⁷ _____ don't we ⁸ _____ home and watch TV?
Gordon: That's a good ⁹ _____. What's on?
Tim: Let me see ... Uh, _Castaway_ with Tom Hanks.
Gordon: ¹⁰ _____!
Tim: And ¹¹ _____ have popcorn, too.
Gordon: ¹² _____ good!

B ▶ 10.4 Listen and check.

LEARN TO respond to suggestions

3A Correct the mistakes in sentences 1–5 and a)–e).

1 Let/ go shopping.   e
2 How about go for a bike ride?
3 Why don't we going to an art gallery?
4 What about staying at home and cook something?
5 Who about making spaghetti and meatballs?

a) That don't sound very interesting. Looking at paintings is boring!
b) I don't really feel like do that. I'm too tired.
c) Sound good. You make the meatballs, I can make the pasta.
d) Brilliant! What would you like eat?
e) That isn't very good idea. I haven't got much money.

B Look at the sentences in Exercise 3A again. Match suggestions 1–5 with responses a)–e).

VOCABULARY weather

4 Add the vowels to the weather words and write them in the correct place in the crossword.

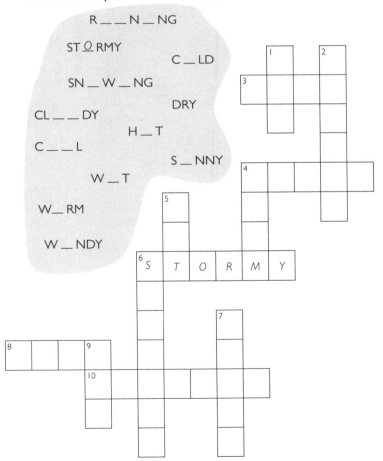

R _ _ N _ NG
ST <u>O</u> RMY
C _ LD
SN _ W _ NG
DRY
CL _ _ DY
H _ T
C _ _ L
S _ NNY
W _ T
W _ RM
W _ NDY

VOCABULARY the body

1A Find twelve words for parts of the body.

S	T	O	M	A	C	H
M	K	T	H	U	M	B
O	N	O	S	E	N	T
U	E	H	F	E	E	T
T	E	E	T	H	C	O
H	H	A	N	D	K	E
F	O	D	B	A	C	K

B ▶ 11.1 Listen and repeat.

C Listen again and write the words in the correct place according to the vowel sound.

I /e/ red	2 /æ/ happy
head	
3 /iː/ meat	4 /əʊ/ no
5 /ʌ/ fun	6 /aʊ/ now

2 Put the letters in order to make health problems. Start with the underlined letter.

1 I feel _sick_ . (ki<u>s</u>c)
2 My leg _____. (<u>sh</u>utr)
3 I've got a bad _____. (<u>ch</u>adeeha)
4 I've got a _____ _____. (ro<u>s</u>e <u>t</u>rahot)
5 My _____ hurts. (delho<u>s</u>ur)
6 I've got awful _____. (ca<u>h</u>ottohe)
7 I've got a _____ _____. (<u>s</u>ero y<u>ee</u>)
8 I feel _____. (b<u>r</u>eritel)
9 I've got a _____. (<u>m</u>etterupare)
10 I've got a _____. (gu<u>c</u>oh)

GRAMMAR should/shouldn't

3A Read the leaflet about travel health. Check any new words in your dictionary.

B Complete the information with *should/shouldn't* and the words in brackets.

TRAVEL HEALTH: BEFORE YOU GO

We answer your FAQs (frequently asked questions) about health on holiday:

1 _Should I see_ (I / see) **my doctor before I go on holiday?**

Yes, 2_____ (*you / speak*) to your doctor or your local travel centre about six weeks before you leave.

3_____ (*I / get*) **any vaccinations?**

Your doctor or nurse can give you information or you can check on the internet. 4_____ (*You / not have*) a lot of vaccinations together, so start early.

What else 5_____ (*I / do*)?

6_____ (*You / visit*) your dentist as well, because dentists can be very expensive in other countries.
7_____ (*You / take*) a Traveller's First Aid Kit with suncream, plasters and painkillers, but 8_____ (*you / not open*) these before you travel. Officials at the airport might ask to check them.

Any other advice?

Well, 9_____ (*you / not travel*) when you have a bad earache or a cold. And it's important to relax, but 10_____ (*you / not drink*) alcohol or coffee in the airport or on the plane, because they'll make you feel worse.

4 Complete the conversation with *should/shouldn't* and a verb from the box. Add the correct pronouns (*I* or *you*).

go (×2)   watch   sleep   do (×2)   change   eat

A: I'm going to fly to Japan soon and I'm worried about the time difference, you know, getting tired after the journey.

B: Oh yes, jet lag can be difficult. 1 _You should go_ to bed early for two or three nights before you travel.

A: What else 2_____?

B: When you're on the plane, 3_____all the food they bring, it's too much. And 4_____ your watch to Japanese local time.

A: And 5_____ on the plane?

B: Yes, you need to rest, so 6_____ all the movies or stay awake the whole time. It's a long journey! What time do you arrive?

A: At two in the afternoon.

B: You'll be very tired, but 7_____ to bed. 8_____ some exercise. It's a good idea to go for a walk and then wait and sleep when it's dark.

A: Thanks. That's good advice.

READING

WALKING – THE PERFECT SPORT?

Forget about tennis, swimming, skiing and jogging. Walking is the easiest and cheapest way to stay fit. It's free, you don't need special clothes or equipment, you don't need a trainer or a special place. Anybody can do it anytime: young people, older people, alone or in groups.

OK – perhaps it's not really a sport, but it IS the most popular physical activity and one of the best ways to stay healthy. What are the benefits? Walking is good for your heart and your legs; regular walkers say they sleep better and feel happier; and smokers say they don't smoke so much.

Maybe you don't have very much time, so here are some ideas to help you start walking:

- Walk, don't drive, to the local shop. If you have a lot to carry, take a small backpack.

- If you have children, walk with them to and from school.

- Get off the bus or train a stop or two early. This will give you some extra daily exercise – and it's cheaper, too!

- Take a walk in your lunch hour at school or work.

- Once a week take a longer walk, and go on a completely new route; this helps to keep things interesting.

There are walkers' clubs all over the world. Join one – walking is a great way to meet people and make new friends!

5A Read the article above and number topics a)–d) in the correct order.

a) Why is walking better than other sports? 1
b) How can you find time for walking?
c) Who can you walk with?
d) Why is walking good for your health?

B Read the article again and tick the ideas the article talks about.

1 Walking isn't expensive. ✓
2 You have to wear good walking shoes.
3 Age isn't important.
4 Walking is good for headaches.
5 You should go shopping on foot.
6 Get up earlier in the morning, and do some extra exercise every day.
7 Take a different walk every week so you don't get bored.
8 You can meet people more easily when walking.

C Find words 1–7 in the text. Then match the words with their definitions a)–g).

1 equipment
2 a trainer
3 alone
4 physical
5 benefits
6 a backpack
7 a route

a) with no other people
b) a bag that you carry on your back
c) connected to your body, e.g. _____ exercise
d) the things you use for an activity, e.g. a machine in the gym
e) a way from one place to another
f) good things
g) a teacher

D Cover the article and try to complete the sentences. Then check your answers with the text.

Maybe you don't have very much time, so here are some ideas to help you start walking:

- Walk, don't drive, ¹_____ the local shop. If you ²_____ a lot to carry, take a small backpack.

- If you ³_____ children, walk ⁴_____ them to and ⁵_____ school.

- Get off the bus or train a stop or two early. This will give you some extra daily exercise – and it's cheaper, ⁶_____!

- Take a walk ⁷_____ your lunch hour ⁸_____ school or work.

- Once a week ⁹_____ a longer walk, and go on a completely new route; this helps to keep things interesting.

There are walkers' clubs ¹⁰_____ over the world. Join one – walking is a great way to ¹¹_____ people and ¹²_____ new friends!

65

VOCABULARY common verbs

1A Complete the diagrams with a verb from the box.

| hear understand ~~forget~~ read run |
| climb swim concentrate remember |

1 *forget*
- a name
- my PIN number
- my ticket

2 _____
- fast
- 800 metres
- down a road

3 _____
- your password
- your mother's birthday
- your first teacher

4 _____
- English
- my teacher
- the problem

5 _____
- a magazine
- a newspaper
- music

6 _____
- a tree
- a mountain
- a tower

7 _____
- a noise
- something outside
- the door close

8 _____
- in a river
- in a lake
- 100 metres

9 _____
- on your homework
- on your work
- on a computer game

B Complete the sentences with verbs from Exercise 1A.

1 I'm too tired and I can't *concentrate*.
2 Sorry, I don't _____. I don't speak Chinese.
3 I can't _____ that! It's too high.
4 Help! Help! I can't _____!
5 I can't _____ this article. Where are my glasses?
6 Don't _____ your keys.
7 Speak up! I can't _____ you.
8 Slow down. We have time and we don't have to _____.
9 I can never _____ my mobile number. I have to write it down.

LISTENING

2A ▶ 11.2 Listen to the radio programme about finding your 'real' age. Number the pictures in the order you hear about them.

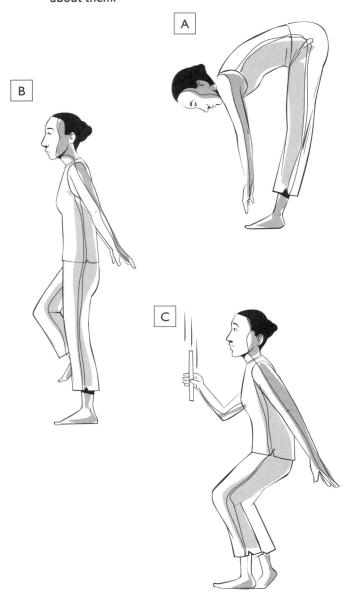

B Listen again and circle the correct information about the interviewer.

1 Her 'birthday' age is _____.
   a) under 20   b) 20–29   c) 30–39

2 Her time (in seconds) for the balance test is _____.
   a) 11–15   b) 16–20   c) 21–25

3 She catches the ruler _____.
   a) near the beginning   b) in the middle   c) at the end

4 She can touch her _____.
   a) toes   b) ankles   c) knees

5 Her real age is _____ her 'birthday' age.
   a) younger than   b) the same as   c) older than

GRAMMAR adverbs of manner

3 Underline the correct alternative.

1 A: Your mum drives really *slow / slowly*.

  B: Yes, well you know that *slow / slowly* drivers don't have many accidents.

2 A: Jeff is quite *lazy / lazily* about doing tasks around the house.

  B: That's true, he does them *lazy / lazily*, but he does them in the end!

3 A: The teacher talks very *quiet / quietly*.

  B: Yes, and the students aren't *quiet / quietly*, so it's difficult to hear.

4 A: I found the shop *easy / easily*, thanks to your clear directions.

  B: Well, in fact, it's rather *easy / easily* to find.

5 A: Our team played *bad / badly* and we lost the match.

  B: That's surprising, I thought the other team was *bad / badly*.

6 A: You're so *energetic / energetically* when you get up in the morning. How do you do it?

  B: I read somewhere that if you get up *energetic / energetically*, you'll feel good all day.

7 A: You came in rather *noisy / noisily* last night.

  B: Sorry, I didn't mean to be so *noisy / noisily*.

8 A: This exercise isn't very *hard / hardly*.

  B: No? Well, work *hard / hardly* to the end because the second part is difficult.

4A Complete the sentences with the adverb form of the words in brackets.

1 You have to drive *carefully* (careful) and _____ (safe). You can't drive _____ (dangerous) or _____ (fast).

2 You have to work very _____ (hard) and often very _____ (late) at night but you get long summer holidays. You don't have to speak _____ (loud), but it helps.

3 You should eat _____ (healthy) and go to bed _____ (early). You don't have to walk or run _____ (fast), but you have to see _____ (clear).

4 You don't have to read music _____ (perfect), but it helps. You have to sing _____ (good), but you don't have to sing _____ (loud).

B Look at the sentences in Exercise 4A again. What are the jobs for each one? Underline the correct alternative.

1 a bus driver / a racing driver

2 a teacher / a politician

3 a footballer / a golfer

4 a jazz singer / an opera singer

5 Complete the sentences with an adjective or adverb.

Conversation 1

A: Are you OK?

B: No, I don't feel very we*ll*_____. Can I lie down somewhere?

A: Yes, over here.

B: I'm really tir_____. I slept terri_____ last night.

Conversation 2

A: This room's very comf_____.

B: Yes, but it's quite noi_____. I can hear the people downstairs.

A: Well, we don't have to stay here all evening. I'm hun_____.

B: Yes, we can eat che_____ in the café tonight and then we can go to that exp_____ Italian restaurant tomorrow.

Conversation 3

A: I sing very ba_____.

B: No, you don't. You sing beau_____.

A: Thank you. That's ki_____ of you.

WRITING adverbs in stories

6A Write the adverbs.

1 slow   *slowly*

2 quick   _____

3 angry   _____

4 nervous   _____

5 careful   _____

B Complete the joke with the adverbs from Exercise 6A.

A man walked [1] *nervously* into the dentist's office. The dentist looked [2] _____ at the man's teeth and then said, 'I have to take one tooth out. I can do it [3] _____ – it'll only take five minutes and it'll cost $100.'

'A hundred dollars for five minutes' work!' the man said [4] _____. 'That's too expensive!'

'Well,' answered the dentist, 'I can do it [5] _____ if you want!'

VOCABULARY problems

1 Complete the conversations with the verbs in the box.

~~cut~~ drop lift stand fall push

1 A: Be careful with that knife!
   B: Why?
   A: You might _cut_ your finger.

2 A: What's the matter?
   B: This box is too heavy. I can't _____ it.

3 A: I can't ride my bike uphill.
   B: So what do you do?
   A: I usually get off and _____ it.

4 A: I can carry these dishes.
   B: Don't carry all of them. You'll _____ them!
   A: I'll be OK. Oh, no!

5 A: It's very windy tonight.
   B: Yes, I think that tree might _____ down.

6 A: Hi, Jenny. It's me.
   B: Hi, Frank. Where are you?
   A: I'm on the train. It's really crowded so I have to _____.

FUNCTION offering to help

2A Put the words in 1–4 and a)–d) in the correct order.

1 my / problem / MP3 / there's / a / player / with
   There's a problem with my MP3 player.

2 favourite / was / that / my / vase
   _____

3 tired / really / I'm
   _____

4 in / cold / here / it's
   _____

a) coffee / let / you / a / make / me
   _____

b) look / me / let
   _____

c) you / I'll / buy / one / another
   _____

d) I / window / shall / close / the?
   _____

B Look at the sentences in Exercise 2A again. Match 1–4 with offers a)–d).

3A Read Jim's 'To do' list. Then use offers of help to complete the conversation.

TO DO
Phone Noriko in Tokyo
Email Moscow office
Get flowers for Ellie – send them to hospital
Meet Anne at airport (5.30)

Ruth: Are you OK, Jim?
Jim: No. I have to meet Anne at 5.30 and look at this list!
Ruth: ¹ _Let_ me _help_ . I'm not busy at the moment.
Jim: Oh, can you? Thanks!
Ruth: No problem. ² _____ I _____ Noriko?
Jim: Yes, please.
Ruth: And then I ³ _____ _____ the Moscow office.
Jim: Can you tell them I'll phone tomorrow?
Ruth: OK. And I ⁴ _____ _____ some flowers for Ellie. I'm going to the hospital to see her tonight anyway.
Jim: Fantastic! ⁵ _____ me _____ you the money.
Ruth: It's OK. Give it to me tomorrow.
Jim: Thanks a lot. I ⁶ _____ _____ the same for you any time!

B  11.3 Listen and check. Then listen and repeat.

LEARN TO thank someone

4 Circle the correct answer.

1 A: Are you OK? Let me carry that.
   B: a) Yes.   b) No problem.   c) Thanks a lot.

2 A: Shall I speak to Mr Chen for you?
   B: a) That's kind of you. b) You're welcome.   c) It's a problem.

3 A: I'll drive you home.
   B: a) You're welcome.   b) Shall I do it?
      c) Thanks. I'm very grateful.

4 A: Thank you very much.
   B: a) Yes.   b) You're welcome.   c) Your welcome.

5 A: Is this seat free?
   B: Sure.
   A: a) Thanks a lot.   b) No problem.   c) You're welcome.

6 A: I'll buy lunch.
   B: a) Really? Please.   b) Really? Sure.   c) Really? Thanks.

VOCABULARY outdoor activities

1A Put the letters in order to make activities. Start with the underlined letters.

1 og hig<u>f</u>ins   _go fishing_
2 cht<u>w</u>a srid<u>b</u>   _____
3 blmi<u>c</u> a no<u>m</u>autni   _____
4 ed<u>r</u>i a sro<u>h</u>e   _____
5 wi<u>sm</u> ni a vi<u>rr</u>e   _____
6 li<u>s</u>a a to<u>ba</u>   _____

B ▶ 12.1 **Listen and check.**

C Listen again and repeat. Write the activities in the correct place according to the stress.

1 oO	2 oOo	3 ooO
	go fishing	
4 ooOo	5 ooooOo	

WRITING postcard phrases

2A Complete the postcard with phrases a)–h).

1 _Verbier_ ,
2 _____
3 _____ ,
4 _____. There's lots of snow so the skiing is perfect. The hotel's beautiful – a little noisy because there's a big group staying here, but it's a lovely old building in the centre of the village. The food's great too – really tasty!

Speaking of food, it's dinner in five minutes so
5 _____!
6 _____ and 7 _____.
8 _____

a) I hope you're all OK
b) I'm having a great time
c) I must go now
d) I'll speak to you soon
e) 5th January
f) ~~Verbier~~
g) Love, Jim
h) Dear Mum and Dad

B Now cross out four unnecessary words in the phrases you wrote in the postcard.

GRAMMAR present perfect

3 Write the past participle of the verbs.

1 be   _been_
2 climb   _____
3 do   _____
4 travel   _____
5 have   _____
6 ride   _____
7 drink   _____
8 play   _____
9 meet   _____
10 fly   _____

4A Look at the table and complete the sentences.

	Ethan	Amy	Tom and Lily
go to South America	✓	✗	✓
see Red Square	✗	✓	✓
eat Mexican food	✗	✓	✗
visit the Louvre gallery in Paris	✗	✗	✓
swim in the Black Sea	✓	✗	✗

1 Ethan _has been_ to South America.
2 Amy _____ to South America.
3 Tom and Lily _____ Red Square.
4 Ethan _____ Red Square.
5 Amy _____ Mexican food.
6 Tom and Lily _____ Mexican food.
7 Tom and Lily _____ the Louvre gallery in Paris.
8 Amy _____ in the Black Sea.

B Complete the questions.
1 _Has_ Ethan _swum_ in the Black Sea?
2 _____ Ethan and Amy _____ the Louvre gallery in Paris?
3 _____ Lily _____ Mexican food?
4 _____ Amy _____ Red Square?
5 _____ Tom and Lily _____ to South America?
6 _____ Tom _____ in the Black Sea?

C Write short answers to questions 1–6 in Exercise 4B.
1 _Yes, he has._
2 _____
3 _____
4 _____
5 _____
6 _____

READING

5A Read Jim's travel blog and write the correct day under each picture.

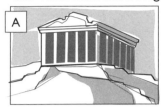

A

Day 1

B

C

D

E

| Destinations | Our Travellers | Forums | Flights | Hotels | Cars | Hostels | Tours | Travel Insurance |

Day 1

We arrived in Piraeus early this morning. Liz has never seen the Parthenon. I've been to Athens once before, so I'm going to be her tour guide. We're going there tonight!

In the afternoon, we went by train from Piraeus into the city of Athens, and walked up to the Parthenon – amazing!

Day 2

Back to Athens again and this time we found a restaurant in the Plaka area. We've eaten Greek food many times back in New Zealand, but this is real Greek food! This is the first time in my life that I've tried octopus and it was delicious!

Day 3

We stayed overnight in Athens and then took a bus down to Cape Sounion in the afternoon to visit the Temple of Poseidon. We've seen many sunsets in our lives, but this was the most beautiful – the sun going down into the Aegean Sea.

Day 4

We left Piraeus early this morning and sailed for twenty hours to the island of Santorini. We arrived in the old port late in the evening. Tomorrow morning we're going up to the village – by donkey! I've ridden horses, camels, and elephants but I've never ridden a donkey!

Day 5

Donkey disaster! I'm writing this from a hospital bed in Athens. We started our donkey ride this morning and I made a big mistake: I walked behind the donkey and it kicked me in the stomach! There was no hospital on the island, so they took me by helicopter to Athens. I've broken three bones ... and I still haven't ridden a donkey. But I *have* flown in a helicopter!

B Read the blog again. Are the sentences true (T) or false (F)?

1 Jim is a tour guide.   F
2 Jim hasn't eaten Greek food before.
3 Jim liked the octopus.
4 They watched the sunrise near the Temple of Poseidon.
5 Jim and Liz travelled to Santorini by boat.
6 Jim enjoyed riding the donkey.
7 Jim flew back to Athens.
8 Now he's back home in New Zealand.

C Correct the false sentences.

1 Jim isn't a tour guide.

_____

_____

_____

_____

6A Imagine it's before the holiday. Read the blog again and write short answers to the questions.

1 Has Liz ever seen the Parthenon?   *No, she hasn't.*
2 Has Jim ever been to Athens?   _____
3 Has Jim ever eaten octopus?   _____
4 Have Jim and Liz ever seen a sunset? _____
5 Has Jim ever ridden a donkey?   _____

B Now imagine it's after the holiday. Read the questions again and write short answers.

1 *Yes, she has.*
2 _____
3 _____
4 _____
5 _____

LISTENING

1A Match activities 1–8 with pictures A–H.

1 go on a roller coaster   *B*
2 get lost
3 be on TV
4 sing in a karaoke club
5 go to the cinema alone
6 fly in a helicopter
7 swim in a lake
8 drive in bad weather

B Complete the quiz with the past participle of the verbs in brackets.

FEAR OR FUN?

Have you ever ...

1 _been_ on a roller coaster? (go)

2 _____ lost in a city? (get)

3 _____ on TV? (be)

4 _____ in a karaoke club? (sing)

5 _____ to the cinema alone to see a film? (go)

6 _____ in a helicopter? (fly)

7 _____ in a lake? (swim)

8 _____ in really bad weather? (drive)

C ▶ 12.2 Listen to four conversations. Which situations from Exercise 1B do the people talk about?

Conversation 1   _6_
Conversation 2   _____
Conversation 3   _____
Conversation 4   _____

D Listen again. Write when the person did the activity.

Conversation 1   _five years ago_
Conversation 2   _____
Conversation 3   _____
Conversation 4   _____

GRAMMAR present perfect and past simple

2 Underline the correct alternatives in conversations 1–3.

Conversation 1

A: ¹*Did you ever fly / Have you ever flown* in a helicopter?

B: No, I ²*didn't / haven't*. ³*Did / Have* you?

A: Yes, I ⁴*did / have*. Just once, when I ⁵*went / 've been* helicopter skiing, five years ago.

Conversation 2

B: ⁶*Have you ever sung / Did you ever sing* in a karaoke bar?

A: No, but I ⁷*sang / 've sung* at a party. It ⁸*was / 's been* last year sometime. No, two years ago. At a birthday party.

A: What ⁹*did you sing / have you sung*?

B: I can't remember ... Oh, yes – 'I Did it My Way'.

Conversation 3

B: ¹⁰*Did you ever drive / Have you ever driven* in really bad weather?

A: Yes. I ¹¹*drove / 've driven* up to Scotland to visit my grandparents in 2007, and it just ¹²*snowed / has snowed* non-stop.

3 Complete the conversations with the correct form of the verbs in brackets.

Conversation 1

A: ¹ *Have you ever ridden* (you / ever / ride) a horse?

B: Yes, I have. I ²_____ (ride) one in Argentina last year.

A: ³_____ (you / like) it?

B: Yes, it ⁴_____ (be) fun, but the horse ⁵_____ (not go) very fast.

Conversation 2

A: Does Emilio go everywhere by motorbike?

B: Yes, he does.

A: ⁶_____ (he / ever / hurt) himself?

B: Yes, he ⁷_____ (break) his arm twice.

A: Really? How ⁸_____ (he / do) that?

B: Both times the weather ⁹_____ (be) bad and he ¹⁰_____ (fall) off the bike.

VOCABULARY prepositions

4 Look at the map and complete the directions with prepositions from the box.

~~through~~   down   up   under   towards
away from   across   over   into   through

Get off the train and walk ¹ *through* the station and ²_____ the steps. There's a big square in front of the station with a clock tower on the other side. Walk ³_____ the square ⁴_____ the clock tower. Walk past the clock tower and go straight on until you see a bridge going ⁵_____ the road. Walk ⁶_____ the bridge and soon you'll see a shopping centre on your left. It's called WhiteWays. Walk ⁷_____ the shopping centre and at the other side you'll come out in Kirkby Street. Walk along Kirkby Street ⁸_____ the shopping centre. Then turn right into Sedgefield Road. My flat is in number thirty-five. The door's usually open so just come ⁹_____ the hall. Walk ¹⁰_____ the stairs to the first floor. My door is the blue one.

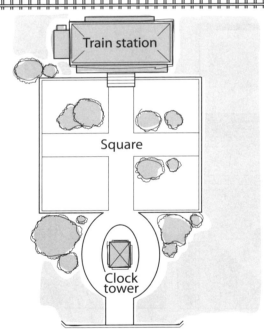

VOCABULARY telephoning expressions

1 Complete Susie's answerphone messages with verbs in the correct form.

1 This is Lisa from the health clinic. I l*eft*_____ a message on your answerphone yesterday. Can you p_____ the clinic, please?

2 Hi, Susie. It's Meg. Can you c_____ me back? I'm at home this evening.

3 Hi. It's me, Bernie. Did you t_____ a message for me last night from Simon?

4 Hello. This is Sports Mad. Can you r_____ us, please? There's a problem with your trainers.

5 Hi, Susie. It's Fallon. I got your message and I'm ph_____ you back.

6 Hi, it's me again. I know you're there! A_____ the phone!

FUNCTION telephoning

2 Tick two correct sentences from telephone conversations. Correct the other six sentences.

1 Just ask ~~she~~ *her* to call me.

2 Could you say me the number?

3 OK, I call you back.

4 Could I leave a message to her?

5 Let me check that.

6 Hi, Frank. I'm Sally.

7 Good morning. Could I chat with Mr Suriano, please?

8 Just a moment.

3 Write the telephone conversations.

Conversation 1

A: Hi, Xavier. This / Bea.
   *Hi, Xavier. This is Bea.*_____

B: Hi, Bea. How / you?
   _____

A: I / OK. Michelle / there?
   _____

B: Yes, but she / sleep.
   _____

A: leave / message / her?
   _____

B: Of course.

A: Just ask / to call / me.
   _____

B: OK. Bye.

Conversation 2

A: Hello. / speak / the manager, please?
   *Hello. Can I speak to the manager, please?*_____

B: Just / moment. I / sorry, he / busy / moment. / call / back later?
   _____

A: It / very important.
   _____

B: I / take / message?
   _____

A: No thanks. I / phone back later.
   _____

LEARN TO say telephone numbers

4A Write the telephone numbers in words. Put a comma between number groups.

1 3234996   *three two three, four double nine six*_____
2 6882975   _____
3 0757281   _____
4 6232889   _____
5 9897766   _____
6 0870 5338992 _____

B ▶ 12.3 Listen and check. Then listen and repeat.

VOCABULARY feelings

5 Complete the adjectives.

1 Don't be a*frai*_____d. I'll go first.

2 Don't be e_____d. Everybody forgets my name.

3 Don't be n_____s. The exam will be easy, I'm sure.

4 Don't be f_____d. It's only a small snake!

5 Well done. I'm very p_____d of you.

6 Don't get e_____d. It isn't a very expensive watch!

GRAMMAR verb forms

1A Complete the article with the correct form of the verbs in brackets. Use the past simple, the present perfect, *would like to* or *be going to*.

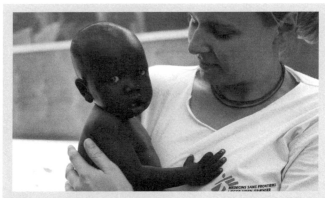

Irish nurse Liz Johnson works with the international aid agency, Médecins Sans Frontières (MSF). She talked to us about her experiences.

'About seven years ago I ¹ *saw* (see) a TV programme about MSF and I ² _____ (decide) to work for them. I ³ _____ (join) MSF three months later.'

'I love my work. I ⁴ _____ (go) to a lot of different places in the world and I ⁵ _____ (meet) some amazing people: doctors, nurses, helpers and patients. In fact, four years ago in Sudan I ⁶ _____ (meet) my husband, Jacques, a French doctor. We now travel and work together. I'm very proud of him.'

Last week Liz and Jacques ⁷ _____ (return) to France after six months work in Haiti. What are their plans for the future? 'We've got some definite plans: Jacques ⁸ _____ (speak) at a big MSF meeting next week and then we ⁹ _____ (have) a one-week holiday in Spain. After that we aren't sure. Next, we ¹⁰ _____ (open) a hospital, but we don't know in which country.'

B Put the words in order to make questions for Liz.

1 did / decide / you / for / when / to / MSF / work?
   When did you decide to work for MSF?

2 you / to / a / have / been / lot / different / of / countries?
   _____

3 meet / you / husband / did / when / your?
   _____

4 to / Jacques / going / week / where / speak / 's / next?
   _____

5 do / you / like / to / next / would / what?
   _____

C Now imagine you are Liz. Answer the questions.

1 *About seven years ago.*

2 _____

3 _____

4 _____

5 _____

VOCABULARY revision

2A Add vowels to the words in each group.

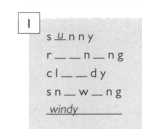

1
s u n n y
r _ _ n _ n g
c l _ _ d y
s n _ w _ n g
windy

2
h _ _ d _ c h _
s _ r _ thr _ _ t
t _ m p _ r _ t _ r _
c _ _ g h
_____

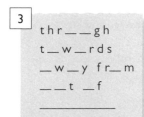

3
thr _ _ gh
t _ w _ rds
_ w _ y fr _ m
_ _ t _ f
_____

4
h _ ngry
th _ rsty
b _ r _ d
l _ st
_____

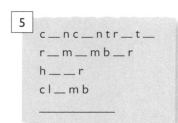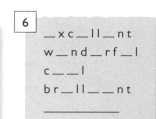

5
c _ nc _ ntr _ t _
r _ m _ mb _ r
h _ _ r
c l _ mb
_____

6
_ x c _ ll _ nt
w _ nd _ rf _ l
c _ _ l
br _ ll _ _ nt
_____

7
sh _ _ ld _ r
kn _ _ _
f _ ng _ r
_ lb _ w
_____

B Match phrases a)–g) with the correct group 1–7 in Exercise 2A.

a) It's ...   *1*
b) The party was ...
c) We got ...
d) Turn left and then walk _____ the car park.
e) I've hurt my ...
f) I've got a ...
g) I can't ...

C Add the words in the box to the correct group in Exercise 2A.

windy   amazing   runny nose   into   understand
sunburnt   thumb

GRAMMAR should/will/might

3A Read the text and write D (Daniel), R (Rebecca) or DR (both) next to problems 1–6.

1 wants to change jobs   *R*
2 works too much
3 lives unhealthily
4 doesn't have any friends
5 is bored with work
6 has money problems

life coaching*

Improve your life and reach your dreams …

Read about two of our customers and how life coaching has helped them:

Daniel is a successful businessman, but he finds it difficult to make friends so at weekends he stays at home and spends a lot of time alone on his computer. On weekdays, he often stays in the office late. He's also overweight and says he's never done much exercise. He'd like to become healthier and go out and meet people, maybe find a girlfriend, but he doesn't know where to start.

Rebecca loves dancing and she teaches a dance class once a week. She works for an electronics company, but she doesn't like her job. She thinks it's boring and works long hours, but she needs the money because her rent is very high. She'd like to teach dance all the time, but she doesn't know how to start.

*coaching = training, teaching

B Read the life-coaching advice and underline the correct alternatives.

66 **Daniel** [1]*should* / *'ll* look for activities he can do with other people. He [2]*should* / *shouldn't* join a club or group, for example a walking club or a cooking group because then he [3]*'ll* / *might* meet people who enjoy the same things. When he's with other people he [4]*should* / *shouldn't* ask them lots of questions and he [5]*should* / *shouldn't* show interest in their answers. People love talking about themselves and they [6]*'ll* / *won't* think he's a great guy! Who knows? He [7]*'ll* / *might* find a girlfriend one day! 99

66 **Rebecca** [8]*shouldn't* / *might* not wait any more. She's in the wrong job. She [9]*should* / *'ll* contact the Association of Dance Teachers – she can find them on the internet and they [10]*might* / *'ll* give her advice about starting a new business. At the moment she [11]*won't* / *shouldn't* leave her job. The best thing is to work part-time, but her company [12]*might* / *might* not agree. She [13]*should* / *shouldn't* start teaching more classes – lots of people want to learn to dance and I'm sure she [14]*won't* / *might not* find it difficult to reach her dream. 99

VOCABULARY Plans

4 Find 12 verb phrases for future plans.

W	T	R	G	R	W	Y	H	I	H
H	A	V	E	A	C	H	I	L	D
A	I	S	T	A	Y	I	N	M	O
V	U	G	M	V	F	D	N	G	S
E	G	O	A	B	R	O	A	D	O
A	O	S	R	G	O	A	S	Z	M
B	F	H	R	G	G	C	T	C	E
A	O	O	I	G	S	O	A	S	S
R	R	P	E	R	P	U	Y	E	P
B	A	P	D	C	E	R	A	S	O
E	W	I	L	R	X	S	T	V	R
C	A	N	A	Z	G	E	H	B	T
U	L	G	E	T	A	J	O	B	B
E	K	Q	S	C	K	X	M	L	X
G	O	F	O	R	A	M	E	A	L

FUNCTION telephoning, offering and suggesting

5A Complete the poem.

'Could I [1] speak to Susie Dee?'
'She's not at [2]h_____. She's back at three.'
Could you [3]p_____ her back tonight?'
'I'll [4]l_____ a message. Is that all right?'
'Just a [5]m_____, I need a pen.'
'She's got my [6]n_____. My name's Ben.'
'[7]L_____ me check, your name is Jack?'
'Oh, never mind – I'll [8]c_____ her back.'

● ● ●

'Well, hello Susie! How are you?'
'I'm fine. What [9]w_____ you like to do?'
'Why [10]d_____ we meet and have a chat?'
'I don't really [11]f_____ like doing that.'
'Then how [12]a_____ a walk together?'
'[13]S_____ good. Let me check the weather.'
It's going to [14]r_____ – that's not ideal.'
'So [15]l_____ stay in and cook a meal!'

B ▶ RC4.1 **Listen to the poem. Then say it with the recording.**

TEST

Circle the correct option to complete the sentences.

1 You dance _____.
  a) beautiful   b) good   c) well

2 A: It's Estelle's birthday on Saturday.
  B: Yes, _____ her a camera. I ordered it last week.
  a) I'm going to give
  b) I'd like to give   c) I give

3 A: Should I tell Felipe?
  B: _____.
  a) Yes, you should tell.
  b) No, you shouldn't.
  c) Yes, you shouldn't.

4 Mack ran quickly _____ Anya and said, 'I'm so happy to see you!'
  a) away from   b) towards   c) across

5 Jan _____ to Germany.
  a) never has been b) was never c) has never been

6 I've got _____.
  a) headache   b) a cough   c) sore throat

7 Have you ever _____ in a thermal spa?
  a) swim   b) swam   c) swum

8 A: Oh, no. A snake!
  B: Don't be afraid. I'm sure it _____ you.
  a) won't hurt   b) 'll hurt   c) might not

9 Hi, _____ Fabio. Is Luigi there?
  a) I'm   b) it's   c) is this

10 A: I feel worse today.
  B: You _____.
  a) should to go home
  b) shouldn't go to bed
  c) should go to bed

11 A: Where _____ in Malta?
  B: At the Carlton Hotel.
  a) you're going to stay
  b) are you going to stay
  c) you would like to stay

12 They _____ yesterday.
  a) 've been fishing b) 've gone fishing
  c) went fishing

13 Peter's very _____ today.
  a) seriously   b) quiet   c) noisily

14 We _____ a great barbecue – about twenty people came.
  a) went   b) had   c) got

15 A: Tom Grady has got a temperature and he _____ says his arms and legs hurt.
  B: I'll phone his mother. I think he's got flu.
  a) also   b) too   c) as well

16 He jumped out of _____.
  a) a helicopter b) a bridge c) an elephant

17 I can't _____ on this test. It's too noisy here.
  a) understand b) concentrate c) remember

18 I always carry lots of water with me so I don't get _____.
  a) dry   b) thirsty   c) hungry

19 Sorry, I can't talk at the moment. Can I _____ in half an hour?
  a) leave a message b) take a message
  c) phone you back

20 I love *Gladiator*. I _____ it about ten times.
  a) saw   b) see   c) 've seen

21 My _____ hurts.
  a) shoulder   b) flu   c) temperature

22 You have to go _____ passport control and security.
  a) out of   b) through   c) into

23 He drove _____ through the city.
  a) fastly   b) slow   c) fast

24 A: What shall we do tonight?
  B: _____ stay in and watch a DVD.
  a) Let's   b) Why we don't
  c) How about

25 A: Did Jake ask you to his wedding?
  B: Yes, but I _____ go because it's in Canada and it's very expensive to fly there.
  a) might   b) might not   c) 'll

26 _____ that for you?
  a) Let me carry b) Shall I carry c) I'll carry

27 Have you ever been to China?
  a) No, I haven't. b) Yes, I have been to.
  c) Yes, I have gone.

28 We _____ get married!
  a) going to   b) 're going to c) 're going

29 I hurt my _____ yesterday and I can't walk.
  a) thumb   b) finger   c) toe

30 I _____ around the world.
  a) 'd like to travel b) 'm like to travel
  c) like travel

TEST RESULT /30

AUDIOSCRIPT

Audio scripts

UNIT 1 Recording 1

1 German, Russian, Mexican, Canadian
2 Polish, Spanish, Scottish
3 Portuguese, Chinese, Japanese
4 Greek, Thai

UNIT 1 Recording 2

1 keys
2 mobile phone
3 passport
4 sunglasses
5 sweater
6 diary
7 magazine
8 laptop
9 newspaper
10 watch
11 ticket
12 camera

UNIT 1 Recording 3

Hello and welcome to *The Travel Programme*. Today's programme is about travelling light. We're at Heathrow Airport in London to ask people about their bags. What's in their hand luggage?

A: Excuse me, sir. Do you have a moment?
B: Oh, er … yes. OK.
A: Can I ask you a couple of questions? First of all, where are you from?
B: I'm from Canada.
A: And are you here on business or are you a tourist?
B: I'm here on business.
A: And can I ask you … what's in your bag?
B: In my bag? Er … let's see. It's a small bag, so not very much. My passport and … plane ticket, my mobile phone, and … let's see … yes, some keys. That's all.
A: Thank you very much.
…
A: Er … excuse me. Can I ask you a couple of questions? It's for the radio.
C: The radio? Oh, OK.
A: Right. Where are you from?
C: I'm French.
A: And are you here on business?
C: No, no, I'm just a tourist.
A: And can I ask you … what's in your bag today?

C: That's a strange question. OK, er … a camera, a newspaper from home – from Paris, my sunglasses … my MP3 player … that's it.
A: And your passport?
C: It's here in my pocket. My passport and money are never in my bag.
A: Thanks very much.
…
A: Excuse me, where are you from?
D: I'm South African. Why?
A: It's for a radio programme. And are you here on business?
D: Yes, yes, on business.
A: And what's in your bag?
D: My bag? Oh, OK. My mobile … laptop … a magazine, sunglasses, a hairbrush … my passport and ticket … and an MP3 player. That's it.
A: Thank you.

UNIT 1 Recording 4

1 These glasses are mine.
2 These keys are yours.
3 That bag is Jack's.
4 Those pencils are mine.
5 This mobile phone is Anita's.
6 That magazine is yours.

UNIT 1 Recording 5

Conversation 1
T = Tourist   S = Shop assistant
T: Excuse me. Do you speak English?
S: Yes. Can I help you?
T: Can I have these four postcards, please?
S: OK. That's two euros, please.

Conversation 2
T = Tourist   W = Waiter
T: Can I have a coffee, please?
W: That's one euro fifty.
T: Thank you.

UNIT 1 Recording 6

A: Hello.
B: Hello. Can I have a tomato salad and a mineral water, please?
A: That's two euros for the salad and one euro for the mineral water.
B: Thanks.

A: Anything else?
B: Er … how much is an ice cream?
A: One euro fifty cents.
B: OK. Can I have an ice cream, too?
C: Hi. How much are the rolls?
B: Which ones?
C: The egg and the chicken.
B: The chicken is two euros seventy cents and the egg is three fifty.
C: And a cheese roll?
B: That's two twenty.
C: OK. Can I have two cheese rolls and an egg roll, please?
B: Anything to drink?
C: Er … yes, three espresso coffees, please.
B: Three espressos at one fifty each. That's four fifty.
C: OK. Thanks.

UNIT 2 Recording 1

key, camera, newspaper, sport, photo magazine, coffee, cinema, exercise MP3 player, DVD, TV, nothing, golf, film

UNIT 2 Recording 2

A: Can I help you?
B: Yes, hi. I'm interested in one of your courses.
A: OK. Which course do you want to do?
B: Er … I don't know. Can you help me?
A: Sure. Well, do you like music?
B: Yes, I do. I listen to music a lot at home, and … I sing in the car sometimes.
A: Then maybe Singing for fun? The class is on Monday and Thursday evenings from six-thirty till eight-thirty at the music school.
B: And what do they do in the classes?
A: Well, the teachers play the guitar and the students er … sing … old songs, new songs. They er …
B: I'm not sure. No … I don't think that's good for me.
A: OK. Let's see … do you take photos?
B: Well, I take them on holiday …
A: … because the Digital photography course is on Saturday

77

mornings from nine to twelve at the high school. A good time if you work Monday to Friday. You study how to take good photos. The teacher is a photographer.

B: Hmmm … no, no, I don't like photography much.

A: Well, do you like dancing? There's a salsa group – Salsa for beginners. They meet at the dance club on Tuesdays and Thursdays from seven to nine and practise salsa dancing. I know that at the weekend they meet and go to dance clubs.

B: Oh, no. I don't dance.

A: Hmmm. OK … Where do you work?

B: At a bank.

A: And do you sit at your desk a lot?

B: Yes, all day. I don't do much exercise.

A: Yes, me too. I'm here all day on the computer but I do Office yoga.

B: What do you do in an Office yoga class?

A: Oh, it's great. We meet here at Union County on Mondays and Wednesdays from seven thirty to nine. We learn exercises that you do at your desk … stretching and relaxing exercises.

B: Yeah. That's good … er … yes … OK, OK. Office yoga. How much is it?

UNIT 2 Recording 3

1 /s/   sleeps, drinks, eats, gets
2 /z/   plays, drives, knows, leaves
3 /ɪz/   relaxes, studies, washes, practises

UNIT 2 Recording 4

1 What time does the train leave?
2 When does the train arrive?
3 What time does the tour start?
4 When does the tour finish?
5 Where does the tour start from?
6 How much does the tour cost?
7 What time does the bank open?
8 When does the bank close?

UNIT 2 Recording 5

Conversation 1

A: Hello, National Rail. Can I help you?

B: Yes, I want to go from London to Cambridge this morning. What time does the next train leave?

A: There's one at 10.52, getting into Cambridge at 11.54.

B: Sorry, could you speak more slowly please? What time does it leave?

A: 10.52.

B: 10.52. That's soon. Er … what time's the next train after that?

A: The next one leaves at 11.15.

B: And when does it arrive in Cambridge?

A: At 12.10.

B: 12.10. Great. Thank you.

Conversation 2

A: Hello.

B: Hello, can I help you?

A: Yes, Can you tell me about the Bangkok temple tour?

B: OK.

A: Er … What time does it start?

B: It starts at 7a.m.

A: 7a.m! That's early. When does it finish?

B: Lunchtime. At about 1 o'clock.

A: OK. And where does it start from?

B: Oh, it starts and ends at the Wat Phra Kaew.

A: Excuse me, the Wat Phra … Er, could you spell that?

B: Sure. W-A-T … P-H-R-A … K-A-E-W.

A: Thanks.

B: Would you like to book the tour?

A: How much does it cost?

B: Six hundred and fifty baht.

A: How much is that in euros?

B: Fourteen euros.

A: OK, yes please.

Conversation 3

A: Hello, National Bank. Can I help you?

B: Yes, just a question about your opening hours. What time do you open on Monday?

A: We open at 9.30 on Monday to Friday.

B: Sorry, could you repeat that? Nine …?

A: Half past nine.

B: And what time do you close?

A: At four.

B: Are you open on Saturdays?

A: Yes, from 10a.m.

B: And what time do you close?

A: At 1p.m.

B: OK, thank you.

UNIT 3 Recording 1

1 kind
2 funny, friendly, stupid, quiet, happy
3 unkind
4 serious, talkative
5 unhappy, unfriendly
6 intelligent

UNIT 3 Recording 2

1	sister	mother
2	cousin	uncle
3	wife	niece
4	aunt	father
5	son	husband
6	grandfather	parents
7	daughter	brother
8	nephew	friend

UNIT 3 Recording 3

M = Meg   D = David

M: OK, Tom. Nice to talk to you. Bye!

D: So who was that?

M: My brother Tom.

D: Oh, have you got a lot of brothers and sisters?

M: No, just one brother and one sister. Tom and Candy.

D: Uh-huh … Do you see them a lot?

M: Well, Tom and I are very close. We often do things together – go to the cinema, play tennis … but I don't see Candy very often. She lives in Scotland and we aren't very close. How about you, David?

D: I'm from a big family. I've got five brothers and a sister.

M: Five! That's a lot of brothers!

D: Yeah, but I don't see them often. Four of them live a long way away. Nick lives here in the city but we hardly ever meet.

M: Why not?

D: Well, he's quite serious and quiet and … well, we like doing different things. He likes staying at home and reading and I … I'm quite active and I like going out.

M: Oh, I see. It's the same for me and Candy. She doesn't like going out, and she isn't very talkative.

D: That makes telephoning a bit difficult.

M: Yeah … so what about <u>your</u> sister?

D: Oh, Jenny and I, we're good friends. We're close. I talk to her a lot … she phones me every day for a chat …usually about <u>her</u> problems.

M: Yeah?

D: Well, she's got a … difficult family situation. Her husband hasn't got a job, they've got three children … no money. You know.

M: Oh. How old are the children?

D: They're very young – two, five and seven. All boys.

M: Wow, three young kids and no money! That's hard.

D: Yes, so we never talk about <u>my</u> life.

M: So she doesn't know about your new job?

D: No, she thinks I'm still a waiter!

M: But you have this great job now! You have to tell her. She's your sister, she'll be happy.

D: Maybe you're right … I don't know, I feel uncomfortable. Ah, that's my phone.

M: Who is it?

D: Oh, it's my sister! Hold on. Hi, Jenny. How are you?

RC1 Recording 1

Group 1
travel
lighter
wallet
Poland
sandwich
waiter

Group 2
newspaper
hairdresser
listen to
credit card
Canada
chewing gum

Group 3
projector
umbrella
accountant
take photos
hot chocolate
Korean

Group 4
engineer
souvenir
clean the rooms
Vietnam
magazine
chicken roll

RC1 Recording 2

Poem 1
I don't like my mobile phone.
I often want to be alone.
But then my mobile phone, it rings.
I really, really hate these things!

Poem 2
'I like cooking and cleaning, too.'
'Oh, good. The guests arrive at two.
You make a cake and wash the floor
and wake me up at half past four!'

Poem 3
'Could I have a sandwich, please?'
'Of course, what kind? Meat or cheese?'
'Oh, I'm not sure, so can I please
have one of those and one of these?'

Poem 4
'Are you free at half past five?'
'Sorry, that's when my friends arrive.'
'Then how about meeting at two or three?'
'Sorry, I'm busy.'
'When are you free?'

RC1 Recording 3

R = Receptionist   G = Guest

R: Can I help you?

G: Hello. My … er … wallet. I … er …

R: Oh, you've lost your wallet? Where did you have it last?

G: I'm sorry, I don't understand. Er … in the restaurant … I … er …

R: No problem. Let me see. What colour is it?

G: Colour? It's … er … brown.

R: And how much money is there in the wallet?

G: Sorry. Could you speak more slowly, please?

R: Erm … how much money is in the wallet?

G: Oh, a hundred dollars and … er … my credit card.

R: OK, let me look. Is this yours?

G: No. No. My wallet's a different brown. Oh, that's mine … yes … in the box.

R: OK, sir. Just a moment. I want to be sure that it's *your* wallet.

G: Of course it's my wallet!

R: Can you tell me anything that's in the wallet?

G: Sorry, could you repeat that?

R: What else is in the wallet?

G: Oh, er … a photo of my wife.

R: OK …

G: … and some money and a credit card.

R: OK. This *is* yours.

G: Thank you!

R: Sorry, just a moment. I need to write some details for our records. Your name is …?

G: Moretti, Vincenzo Moretti.

R: That's M-o-double r?

G: No, one r and double t.

R: M-o-r-e-t-t-i … and your room number, Mr Moretti?

G: 368.

R: Have you got a mobile phone number?

G: Yes, it's 03837 4025.

R: … 4125.

G: No, 4025.

R: OK, thank you. Please sign here.

G: All right … Oh, what's the date?

R: Today's the ninth of April.

G: Ninth … April … 2011. OK, thank you very much!

R: Mr. Moretti?

G: Yes?

R: Is this your keycard?

G: Oh, oh yes! Thank you!

UNIT 4 Recording 1

1 Is there a <u>living</u> room?
2 There's a big <u>kitchen.</u>
3 Is there a <u>television</u>?
4 How many <u>people</u> are there?
5 There are <u>two</u> of us.
6 There's a large <u>shopping</u> centre.

UNIT 4 Recording 2

I = Interviewer   J = Janet

I: So, Janet, tell us about your holidays.

J: OK. Well, every year I take a week's holiday in Spain … I stay in a beautiful villa, I have three meals a day, I have a lovely room, and I meet a lot of new people.

I: That sounds nice … but very expensive!

J: No, it's free – it costs me nothing.

I: Why's that?

J: Well, it's called Pueblo Inglés, or English village, and it's a place where Spanish people go to practise their English. So the Spanish people are the students, and they pay, but the English speakers pay nothing – we just speak English all day with the students.

I: Really? How many people are usually there? And where are they all from?

J: There are usually about twenty English speakers from Canada, the USA, England, Australia and Ireland, and twenty Spanish people from all over Spain.

I: Are they all in their twenties, like you?

J: Well, there are a lot of different ages, from early twenties to about sixty.

I: And what do you do on a typical day?

J: We have breakfast and then we do things together in pairs – an English speaker and a Spanish speaker. After fifty minutes, we have a ten-minute break and then we go with a different person. We do different activities and we speak English all day. In the evening we have a big meal together. There's only one rule. No Spanish! It's great fun – I love it!

I: It sounds great. Thanks, Janet. If you want to find out more about Pueblo Inglés, there's information on our website at …

UNIT 5 Recording 1

1 milk   chicken
2 meat   bread
3 cucumber   onion
4 sausages   hot dog
5 sardines   carrots
6 banana   grape
7 yoghurt   butter
8 fruit   juice

UNIT 5 Recording 2

1 two thousand, five hundred and twenty-three
2 three thousand, one hundred and forty-five
3 one thousand, one hundred and one
4 ten thousand
5 seven hundred and twenty-one
6 two hundred and fifty thousand

UNIT 5 Recording 3

I = Interviewer   M = Mike

I: Welcome to *Twenty-four seven* – the programme about people and lifestyle. Today we're talking to Dr Mike McKay, who wrote the bestseller *The Junk food lover's diet.* So Dr McKay, is it true that on your diet, I can eat anything I want?

M: Yes, that's right.
I: I can eat junk food – hamburgers, pizza, chips, crisps, chocolate …
M: It's all fine. You can eat anything you want, and you'll lose weight.
I: Well … can you explain that?
M: It's very simple. You can eat anything but you can't eat too much. So go ahead, get a hot dog every week … but don't eat the whole thing! Eat half of it.
I: Oh, I see. So with chocolate, for example, how much is not too much?
M: Well, everybody loves chocolate. One bar a day is too much. On the Junk food lover's diet, you can eat two bars a week – no more.
I: This sounds great! How about pizza? How much pizza is OK on the Junk food lover's diet?
M: For lunch, you can have one piece of pizza.
I: Every day?
M: Every day.
I: I usually eat four or five!
M: Well, that's too much. On the Junk food lover's diet, you can eat anything … but not too much.
I: Is it OK to have pizza for dinner?
M: Well, pizza is very rich … so have pizza at lunchtime, eat light foods for dinner.
I: OK, crisps are light but surely they're bad … so full of oil and salt.
M: Well, one big packet of crisps every day, that's too much of course. But you can have three packets in a week.
I: So Monday, Wednesday and Friday are crisp days!
M: Oh, OK!
I: How many hamburgers can I eat?
M: One.
I: One a day, that's not bad …
M: One a week! You can have one hamburger a week in a roll, with ketchup and cheese – that's all fine.
I: And a diet cola?
M: Or a regular cola.
I: Really, cola with sugar …
M: Yup, but …
I: …not too much!

UNIT 5 Recording 4

1 I'd like a hamburger with onion and tomato in a roll and some salad, please.
2 Could I have a veggie burger with corn on the cob? And some onions on the burger, please.
3 Can I have a hamburger in a roll with lettuce and onion? And a salad too, please.

UNIT 5 Recording 5

1 and a salad too, please
2 corn on the cob
3 and some onions on the burger
4 a hamburger in a roll
5 with onion and tomato
6 with lettuce and onion

UNIT 6 Recording 1

The nineteenth of March, 1959
October the thirtieth, 1995
The thirty-first of March, 2002
January the sixth, 1805
The thirteenth of October, 1957
The twenty-first of May, 1910
January the twenty-sixth, 2005

UNIT 6 Recording 2

/t/	/d/	/ɪd/
worked	changed	started
finished	loved	wanted
stopped	played	hated
helped	tried	
	enjoyed	
	travelled	

UNIT 6 Recording 3

thought, met, spoke, grew, woke, taught, knew, drew, wrote, slept, left, bought

UNIT 6 Recording 4

P = Philip   D = Denise

P: Well, we haven't got any children so we adopted Zsilan in 1999. We went to China … and we met Zsilan there and we brought her home with us to Sydney. She was, er, about two years old, but at first there was a problem …
D: Yes, she was a very intelligent little girl, but at first she was also

really quiet. She ate a lot … but she didn't talk much … we didn't know what to do.

P: Yes, she was very unhappy.

D: So we went on the internet and we looked for other families with adopted Chinese children … and we found a website and well, we got a big surprise.

P: Yes, we wrote about Zsilan on the website. We wrote about her birthday – that it was on May 8th …

D: … and a woman in Melbourne wrote back to say that *her* daughter, also a Chinese girl, named Lin, had the same birthday!

P: So we put a photo of Zsilan on the website, and this other woman put up a photo of Lin, and …

D: Here are the photos. Look at them. The girls look exactly the same.

P: Yes, so we started to think, yes, maybe they *are* sisters … maybe they're twins. So we went to Melbourne with Zsilan and the two little girls met …

D: It was amazing, from the first moment! They looked at each other with such love, and then they laughed and played together all day.

P: For the first time, I felt that Zsilan was really happy.

D: We were sorry to leave. Zsilan and Lin never lived together but they visit each other a lot and they like the same things: dancing and swimming …

P: A year ago, when the girls were eight years old, we had tests, and it was true – they *are* sisters! And with the same birthday, of course they're twins.

D: When we told Zsilan that Lin really was her sister, she smiled and said, 'I *know* she's my sister.'

UNIT 6 Recording 5

P = Philip   D = Denise

P: She was, er, about two years old, but at first there was a problem …

D: Yes, she was a very intelligent little girl but at first she was also really quiet. She ate a lot … but she didn't talk much … we didn't know what to do.

P: Yes, she was very unhappy.

UNIT 6 Recording 6

Conversation 1
A: What did you do on Saturday?
B: I had lunch with my grandparents.
A: That sounds nice.

Conversation 2
A: Did you have a good day yesterday?
B: No, we went for a walk and it rained!
A: So what did you do?

Conversation 3
A: Did you have a good weekend?
B: I wasn't very well so I stayed in bed.
A: That sounds awful.

Conversation 4
A: How was your weekend?
B: Fantastic, thanks!
A: Why, what did you do?

Conversation 5
A: Did you do anything special at the weekend?
B: No, we just stayed at home and relaxed.
A: That sounds lovely.

RC2 Recording 1

1 The oranges are next to the bread.
2 The cheese is between the beans and the pasta.
3 The pasta is under the rice.
4 The apples are on the left of the oranges.
5 The grapes are behind the carrots.
6 The bread is above the grapes and carrots.
7 The apples are between the rice and the oranges.
8 The beans are on the left of the carrots.

UNIT 7 Recording 1

1 empty
2 noisy
3 cheap
4 boring
5 uncomfortable
6 slow
7 expensive
8 quiet
9 fast
10 comfortable
11 crowded
12 interesting

UNIT 7 Recording 2

Hello, it's 9.48a.m. on Monday the second of December. I'm Nick Young and I'm on the Trans-Siberian train. Welcome to my audio diary. First of all, some facts: the Trans-Siberian is the longest train journey in the world. It's 9,300 kilometres and takes seven days …

…

So, this is day one – we left the city an hour ago and I'm here in my compartment. It's quite comfortable with two beds, one for me and one for Anton. Anton's from Sweden and he's very friendly. He doesn't speak much English but that's not a problem.

…

Hi, Nick here. It's day three and we're in Siberia. Out of the window you can see snow and forests and small villages for kilometre after kilometre. It's beautiful. About every two hours the train stops at a small station and there are women selling bread, fish, fruit or vegetables. We often buy food for lunch or dinner. When we get back on the train, we chat and read and have more cups of tea. Then we have lunch and then dinner and then we go to bed. It's all very relaxing.

…

Hi there. This is my last audio diary on this journey. In one hour we get into Vladivostok station! Last night the Russian lady in the carriage next door had her fiftieth birthday party. It was crowded but we had a good time!

So what do I think about the Trans-Siberian train? Fantastic! And my best memories? Great dark forests, small Russian villages, and some good new friends. I really think this is the best journey of my life!

…

UNIT 7 Recording 3

Conversation 1
A: So, the park's between the cinema and the pharmacy.
B: No, it's behind the cinema and the pharmacy.

Conversation 2
A: So the supermarket's between the cinema and the pharmacy.
B: No, it's between the cinema and the post office.

Conversation 3
A: So, the cinema is the fourth building on the left.
B: No, it's the third building on the left.

Conversation 4
A: So, the café is the fourth building on the left.
B: No, it's the fourth building on the right.

Conversation 5
A: So, the post office is opposite the bank.
B: No, it's opposite the museum.

Conversation 6
A: So, the town hall is opposite the bank.
B: No, it's next to the bank.

UNIT 8 Recording 1

1 Hello … Oh, hi Rob … No, we're at the new exhibition at the National Gallery and we're looking at the Klimt paintings … Yeah, they're fantastic … OK, see you later.
2 Nellie, it's me, Russ … Hi, yeah, we're queuing to buy tickets for the concert. Do you want to come? I can get you a ticket … Two…? Oh, who's your new friend … ? Right. See you soon.
3 Hi … Oh, look, I can't talk now – we're just going in to a concert … It's the Mozart … Yeah, the Requiem … Sorry, I've got to go.
4 Hi, Felicity … Fine, thanks … Listen, do you want to have a coffee later … ? After the match – maybe around four o'clock … Yeah, it's Nadal again – he's amazing … Oh, you're watching the match on TV … ? Right, see you at four.
5 Zsuzsa, I just had to call you. The new designs, they're fantastic – everything's black and white, you know. Kate's wearing white and Fabio's in all-black – black jeans, a black sweater and black jacket … OK, yeah, I'll take some pictures … Talk to you later.

UNIT 8 Recording 2

1 Are you looking for a film?
2 Is it an action film?
3 Is anyone famous in it?
4 Do you want to borrow a DVD?
5 I haven't got a DVD player
6 I've got it on video.

UNIT 8 Recording 3

1 Are you looking for a friend?
2 Is it an action film?
3 Is anyone famous in it?
4 Do you want to buy a DVD?
5 I haven't got a CD player.
6 I've got it on video.

UNIT 9 Recording 1

1 fast
2 healthy
3 dangerous
4 inconvenient
5 difficult
6 convenient
7 safe
8 easy
9 comfortable
10 polluting

UNIT 9 Recording 2

R = Reporter C = Carin
R: We're in Amsterdam, the Netherlands, and we're talking to Carin van Buren. Carin's riding a kind of scooter with a motor. Carin, what is this … er … machine called?
C: It's a balancing scooter.
R: And do you ride it around the city?
C: Yes, I use it to go to work. Before this year I went to work by bike or sometimes by bus. Then I saw a balancing scooter on the internet and thought, that looks good, and I bought one!
R: Is it difficult to ride?
C: No, it's actually very easy.
R: And how long does it take to learn to ride?
C: It takes about two hours. Yes, it took me two hours.
R: Can you ride it on the pavement here?
C: No, you can't. You have to ride it on the road or you can use the bike paths.
R: And how fast does it go?
C: The maximum speed is twenty-five kilometres an hour but I usually go slower than that.
R: Do you feel safe on it?
C: Yeah – yes, I do. I always wear a helmet. The scooter doesn't go very fast and it's easy to stop.
R: And is it better than travelling by bus or bike?
C: I think so. By bus it took about forty-five minutes to go to work and now it takes me twenty minutes by scooter. And it's better than a bike because I'm not hot when I arrive at work.
R: Where do you leave your scooter at work?
C: I take it into my office and I leave it near my desk.
R: Really?
C: Yeah, it isn't a problem.
R: Is it tiring to ride?
C: Yes, it is quite tiring. You can't really relax.
R: Is there anything else you don't like about the scooter?
C: Sometimes people laugh at me and I feel quite stupid. Oh yes, and people often stop me and ask questions about it! I don't like that.

UNIT 9 Recording 3

A: Oh, hi. I'm really sorry I'm late. I missed the train.
B: I don't believe you.
A: No, really, the traffic was terrible.
B: And?
A: And my car broke down.
B: Your car, again?
A: And I left my wallet at home.
B: Ah, your wallet.
A: And … OK, I forgot about our meeting! I feel terrible about this.
B: Well, don't worry about it.
A: I'm so sorry …
B: No, really, it's fine.
A: I'm so so …
B: That's OK!! But don't let it happen again.

RC3 Recording 1

G = Greg J = Jurgen
G: Hey, Jurgen. It's my wife's birthday tomorrow. Can you recommend a good restaurant?
J: Well, what kind of food do you like?
G: We both like Chinese food and … er … French food.

J: There's a good restaurant called *Bouchon* in town. It serves French food.

G: Do you think my wife would like it?

J: Yes, I think so. It's quite romantic.

G: Where is it?

J: It's in a small street near the cinema.

G: Can you tell me the way?

J: From the cinema, you go down Hillside Road past the pharmacy and turn left.

G: Left at the pharmacy. OK …

J: Then go straight on for about two hundred metres. Take the second right and *Bouchon* is on the right. It isn't far.

G: Great – thanks!

…

J: Hi, Greg. Did you find the restaurant?

G: No!

J: Oh? Why?

G: Your directions were all wrong! You said to turn *left* at the pharmacy.

J: Oh, no …

G: And we did, but it took us completely the wrong way!

J: Oh, no – I'm so sorry. I always mix up left and right.

G: Hm. My wife was really angry.

J: I feel terrible about this.

G: In the end we went home and ordered pizza!

J: Oh, no …

G: Ah, well. Maybe next year! Don't worry about it, really.

UNIT 10 Recording 1

sunburnt, thirsty, bored, wet, hungry, hot, lost, cold

UNIT 10 Recording 2

Speaker 1

Well, the most difficult thing was that there was so much water, but I was so thirsty. Food wasn't a big problem because I caught fish and ate them. Of course I got sunburnt after the first day because I had nothing to put on my head. And I was afraid of sharks – once I saw one, but it just swam around the raft for a few minutes and then it went away.

Speaker 2

I felt very small and very tired. I walked all night, very slowly because of the sand, and I tried to stay cool in the daytime, but it was so hot. On the second day I found some water – that was very lucky – but then I wanted to walk more, not just stay by the water. I wanted to try to find my way back to the town. I had food with me, so I didn't get hungry – just very thirsty. Once I saw a snake, and I was afraid that one might go into my shoe, so I never took my shoes off.

Speaker 3

There was snow everywhere, everything was white, and that's why I got lost – I didn't see the path. I was up there only one night, but it was the longest night of my life. The most important thing was staying warm. I didn't have enough clothes with me, so I got terribly cold. I wanted to make a fire, but everything was wet. I slept on the ground and got colder. I didn't think about food, I wasn't really hungry, but just so thirsty … it was difficult, very difficult.

Speaker 4

There was water, so I didn't get thirsty. And I didn't get too hungry because I knew what kind of plants to eat. Of course I got very lost, I walked day and night … but you know you can never, ever get bored there. There are so many different types of plants and animals and insects, it was beautiful … so yes, I felt tired and lost, but not bored.

UNIT 10 Recording 3

1 You get cold.
  You'll get cold.

2 We'll miss the train.
  We miss the train.

3 I'm sure you'll hate it.
  I'm sure you hate it.

4 They know you're a tourist.
  They'll know you're a tourist.

5 I stay at home.
  I'll stay at home.

6 I'll never go out.
  I never go out.

UNIT 10 Recording 4

T = Tim   G = Gordon

T: So, Gordon, what would you like to do today?

G: I don't know. Have you got any ideas?

T: What about going to a concert?

G: Hmmm … That might be difficult.

T: Why?

G: We don't like the same music. You like rock, I like hip-hop.

T: Oh. That's true. How about inviting some friends?

G: I don't really feel like doing that.

T: OK then. Why don't we stay home and watch TV?

G: That's a good idea. What's on?

T: Let me see … Uh, *Castaway* with Tom Hanks.

G: Brilliant!

T: And let's have popcorn, too.

G: Sounds good!

UNIT 11 Recording 1

head, toe, neck, teeth, hand, knee, feet, mouth, back, nose, thumb, stomach

UNIT 11 Recording 2

I = Interviewer   A = Adrian

I: In today's programme I'm at the Real Age Clinic with Doctor Adrian Clark. Adrian, how can I find out my 'real' age?

A: OK, how old are you?

I: I'm thirty-one.

A: OK. We call that your 'birthday' age. Right. I'm going to ask you to do some tests and then I can tell you if your real age is younger or older than thirty-one.

I: OK.

A: We'll start with three simple tests. First of all is the Balance Test. Come over here, please. OK, you have to close your eyes and stand on one leg.

I: Stand on one leg. Right.

A: And I'm going to time you.

I: Whoa … this is quite difficult. I feel a bit stupid. I wasn't very good at that. How long was it?

A: You did fourteen seconds.

I: That isn't very good, is it?

A: Well, most people under twenty find this test easy but not many people over thirty can stand on one leg for more than twenty-five seconds. The average for your age is about fifteen to twenty seconds … so fourteen seconds is OK.

I: Right. What's the next test?

A: The second test is the Ruler Test. Which hand do you write with?

I: My right hand.

A: OK, hold out your right hand and open your thumb and first finger. I'm going to hold this ruler above your hand. I'll say 'now' and you have to catch it.

I: OK.

A: Are you ready?

I: Yes.

A: Now … Oh, well done. You caught it … in the middle.

I: Is that good?

A: Yes, at twenty you should catch the ruler half way down – in the middle. People over forty-five don't usually catch it!

I: Oh, good … that's better.

A: And the next test. Can you touch your toes?

I: Yes, that's easy.

A: Ah, yes – but you have to keep your legs straight.

I: Ah. I can touch my knees … and …

A: No, be careful. Go slowly. That's enough. You can touch your ankles. That's quite good for your age.

I: So … how did I do?

A: Not bad. Your 'real' age from these three tests is … twenty-nine. Now I'm going to ask you some questions about your lifestyle and general health.

UNIT 11 Recording 3

A: Are you OK, Jim?

B: No. I have to meet Anne at 5.30 and look at this list!

A: Let me help. I'm not busy at the moment.

B: Oh, can you? Thanks!

A: No problem. Shall I phone Noriko?

B: Yes, please.

A: And then I'll email the Moscow office.

B: Can you tell them I'll phone tomorrow?

A: OK. And I'll get some flowers for Ellie. I'm going to the hospital to see her tonight anyway.

B: Fantastic! Let me give you the money.

A: It's OK. Give it to me tomorrow.

B: Thanks a lot. I'll do the same for you any time!

UNIT 12 Recording 1

1 go fishing
2 watch birds
3 climb a mountain
4 ride a horse
5 swim in a river
6 sail a boat

UNIT 12 Recording 2

Conversation 1

A: Have you ever flown in a helicopter?

B: No, I haven't. Have you?

A: Yes, I have. Just once, when I went helicopter skiing – five years ago.

B: That sounds interesting. What's helicopter skiing?

A: A helicopter takes you up the mountain and you ski from there.

B: And how was it?

A: It was fun. I enjoyed it.

Conversation 2

A: Matt, have you ever sung in a karaoke club?

B: No, but I've sung at a party. It was last year sometime. No, two years ago. At a birthday party.

A: What did you sing?

B: I can't remember … Oh, yes – *I Did It My Way*. It was fun. I can't sing, but it was a good laugh. Why are you asking?

A: I'm going to a karaoke club tonight and I'm feeling quite nervous about it.

B: You'll be all right. Just relax and enjoy it!

Conversation 3

A: What's the matter?

B: I have to drive to Dublin tomorrow and look at the rain! Have you ever driven in really bad weather?

A: Yes. I drove up to Scotland to visit my grandparents in 2007 and it just snowed non-stop – it was impossible to see the road ahead.

B: Sounds dangerous.

A: Yes, so I stopped and stayed overnight in a hotel. After that I always visit them by train!

B: Yeah, that's a good idea. Maybe I'll go by train.

Conversation 4

A: Look at this picture. It looks scary! Have you ever been on a roller coaster like that?

B: Yes, when I was about nineteen in Munich. A friend of mine took me on a really big roller coaster.

A: Were you afraid?

B: No. After ten seconds I closed my eyes and didn't open them until it stopped!

UNIT 12 Recording 3

1 three two three, four double nine six

2 six double eight, two nine seven five

3 oh seven five, seven two eight one

4 six two three, two double eight nine

5 nine eight nine, double seven double six

6 oh eight seven oh, five double three, eight double nine two

RC4 Recording 1

A: Could I speak to Susie Dee?

B: She's not at home. She's back at three.
Could you phone her back tonight?

A: I'll leave a message. Is that all right?

B: Just a moment, I need a pen.

A: She's got my number. My name's Ben.

B: Let me check, your name is Jack?

A: Oh, never mind – I'll call her back.

A: Well, hello Susie! How are you?

C: I'm fine. What would you like to do?

A: Why don't we meet and have a chat?

C: I don't really feel like doing that.

A: Then how about a walk together?

C: Sounds good. Let me check the weather.
It's going to rain – that's not ideal.

A: So let's stay in and cook a meal!

Pearson Education Limited
Edinburgh Gate
Harlow
Essex CM20 2JE
England
and Associated Companies throughout the
world.

www.pearsonlongman.com

© Pearson Education Limited 2011

First published 2011
Third Impression 2011

ISBN: 978-1-4082-5946-7

Set in Gill Sans Book 9.75/11.5
Printed in Slovakia by Neografia

Acknowledgements
Text permissions

We are grateful to the following for permission
to reproduce copyright material:

Text
Extract Chapter 5 adapted from "Do you eat
to live or do you live to eat?" Anita Nagy blog
7 September 2006, http://www.bbc.co.uk/
worldservice/learningenglish/communicate/blog/
student/0000007386.shtml, reproduced with
permission from Anita Nagy; Extract Chapter 8
adapted from "History of the T-shirt", www.t-
shirt-buyers-guide.org, copyright © T-Shirt-
Buyers-Guide.org; Extract Chapter 10 adapted
from "Teenage lottery winner: 'So which bank
should I trust with my £7m jackpot?'", Daily
Mail, 1 October 2008 (Hull, L.), copyright ©
Solo Syndication 2008.

In some instances we have been unable to trace
the owners of copyright material, and we would
appreciate any information that would enable us
to do so.

The publisher would like to thank the following
for their kind permission to reproduce their
photographs:

(Key: b-bottom; c-centre; l-left; r-right; t-top)

6 Photolibrary.com: Corbis (bl). 10 Photolibrary.
com: Purestock (tl). 12 Getty Images: Stephen
Mallon (br). 17 Jupiter Unlimited: Stockxpert
(br). 18 Photolibrary.com: White (tr). 20 Jupiter
Unlimited: Stockxpert (tr). 24 Photolibrary.com:
Niall McDiarmid/Red Cover (t). 25 Courtesy of
Pueblo Inglés: courtesy of Pueblo Ingles (tr). 31
Getty Images: Paul Visconti/StockFood Creative
(tl). 32 Photolibrary.com: Yvette Cardozo/Index
Stock Imagery (cl). 34 Rex Features: Chris
Weeks/BEI (tl). 35 Getty Images: Ian Cook/
Time & Life Pictures (cl). 36 Getty Images:
Photodisc/SD Productions (tc). 41 Getty Images:
Michelle Pedone (br). 42 iStockphoto: (br). 44
Jupiter Unlimited: Goodshoot (tr). 49 Alamy
Images: Photos 12 (cr). Getty Images: Tom
Schierlitz (tr/Suit). Jupiter Unlimited: Stockxpert
(tl/Jeans) (tl/Socks) (tr/Coat) (tr/Jacket) (tl/
Shirt) (tr/Trousers) (tl/Shoes) (tr/Jumper) (tl/
Dress) (tr/Skirt) (tr/Top). shutterstock: Elnur
(tl). 52 Getty Images: Ghislain & Marie David
de Lossy (c). 54 Photolibrary.com: Huntstock
(tr). 56 Alamy Images: Natalie Jezzard (tc).
60 Press Association Images: Dave Thompson
(cl). 62 Corbis: Radius Images (br). 65 Jupiter
Unlimited: Photos.com (tr). 74 Medecins Sans
Frontieres: Mikkel Dalum (tl) (the picture shown
is not 'Liz Johnson' but a generic MSF worker)

All other images © Pearson Education